MARY QUEEN OF SCOTS By H. T. SKAE

MARY QUEEN OF SCOTS

M A R Y
QUEEN OF SCOTS
BY HILDA T. SKAE

T. N. FOULIS
LONDON & EDINBURGH
1912

Published November 1912

Printed by Morrison & Gibb Limited, *Edinburgh*

THE LIST OF CHAPTERS

THE LIST of ILLUSTRATIONS

THE LIST of ILLUSTRATIONS

INTRODUCTION

MARY QUEEN OF SCOTS
INTRODUCTION

AMONG THE NAMELESS GENERA-
tions who swarm and succeed each other
upon this earth there occurs from time
to time an individual who leaves a mark
never to be forgotten or effaced, whose
vitality has been so strong that it agitates
mankind in the form of questioning and
debate so long as the race endures. The
tale and personality of Mary Stewart are
among those which remain eternally fascinating; her beauty, brilliancy, and charm
seeming to pierce through the dark of
ages, while her story is perhaps the most
romantic and poignant in history. Her figure still stands out vividly among a throng
of others that have become dim and ob-
scure. Thinking or reading of her, we seem
at times to see her features and hear the
very tones of her voice; then again the mystery recurs. What was her real character?
how did she bear herself in certain crises
regarding which we have only imperfect
knowledge?

3

MARY QUEEN OF SCOTS

No man can tell ; each fills in the outlines according to his own ideas and temperament, and reconstructs the story in his own way. No one having fallen under the spell can escape from it, but seems to be following an elusive figure, now bright with the full light of history, now dim with mysterious clouds—fascinating, alluring, baffling. So clear does the figure become that it seems as though one had but to approach and look into the eyes in order to see what historians have omitted to tell ; then the vision fades, and the mystery remains as impenetrable as ever.

Rightly to understand Mary Stewart, it is necessary to follow her career from earliest childhood and through varying scenes—see her sheltered and idolised in France, frowned upon and threatened in Scotland, surrounded by Elizabeth's spies, and with pitfalls ready for her feet. There is no lack of contemporary accounts and descriptions, but the story always remains incomplete in the critical part. Follow-

4

THE DAUPHIN OF FRANCE

ing her so far, we are convinced that she is sweet and sunny in disposition, brave, gay, audacious; a poet and lover of what is chivalrous and romantic; tender-hearted, as is shown by a thousand proofs; outspoken, true to her friends, and, we cannot doubt, sincere. We see her tempted and sorely tried, and she bears the test; then a disaster occurs, a disaster which stuns and paralyses; and when the noise and turmoil have died down, and the smoke has cleared away from a building treacherously blown up by gunpowder, leaving blackened ruins and corpses, we are asked to believe that a woman possessing these qualities has lured her husband to his death by assassination.

What was her share in the proceedings? Was she innocent, while made by cunning plots to appear guilty? Or did this noble nature break down under the strain of temptation, warped by violence and disappointment, and take the most ready and violent means of escape from the difficulty?

5

MARY QUEEN OF SCOTS

Thus the eternal question recurs until the Queen becomes the most living figure in history, so vivid and importunate that she must actually be loved or hated. With regard to her there is no middle course.

CHAPTER THE FIRST
THE HOPE OF SCOTLAND

MARY OF GUISE
Queen of James V.

CHAPTER THE FIRST
THE HOPE OF SCOTLAND

SEVEN GENERATIONS OF STEW-
art kings had inherited the throne of Scotland, and each, save one, had been cut off
by a sudden and violent death or had sunk
under the troubles and calamities of his
reign. Yet each in his turn had set out
with fresh hope; theirs was no craven race,
and none had let himself be intimidated
by the fate of his predecessor. Certain well-
defined characteristics run through the
line : all were vigorous and full of the joy
of living ; a love of poetry and of the arts
distinguished them all—of fighting, hunting, and manly exercises ; and in the pursuit of glory or pleasure they were heedless
of consequence.

All these characteristics were united in
James v., with perhaps a reinforced strain
of gaiety and recklessness. In times when
a new order of things had dawned, he was
still a mediæval knight. He lived his
life to the full, and proved strong enough
to enforce order among his turbulent sub-

9

jects : cruel he had shown himself to be under great provocation, but he was loved by the poor, and won the surname of "The King of the Commons." Another Haroun al-Raschid, he moved freely in disguise among all classes—nobles, burghers, peasants, true men, and outlaws. He learned much and had many strange adventures in the character of "The Gudeman of Ballengeich." He made love, lawful and lawless, and married two French princesses in succession. He allied himself with France, and defied his uncle Henry VIII. of England ; then, when motives of chivalry and wounded pride prompted, he rushed into war with full confidence in the righteousness of his cause.

In December 1542 he lay dying in Falkland Palace. His nobles had deserted him at Fala Moor ; had refused to follow their king into battle against the hereditary foe. Three weeks later had followed the terrible disaster of Solway Moss, and James, crushed by shame and disappoint-

ment, had dragged himself northward to Edinburgh and thence to Falkland, where he remained, his forces too spent to go further.

All his schemes had failed; his nobles were against him, and his favourite, Oliver Sinclair, had been responsible for the ignominious rout of his followers by the English.

"My portion in this world is spent," said the King. His two sons were dead, and there now remained only one hope—that the child about to be born in Linlithgow Palace might be a boy.

Then came the news of a daughter's birth.

"The deil go with it," muttered James, thinking that his line was at an end; "it came with a lass and it will go with a lass," and he would not send the child his blessing.

"Fie, fled, Oliver," he crooned; and he "turned his back on his lords and his face to the wall."

When the end came near, he gave " ane little laughter," kissed his hand to his lords, and passed away, a little more than thirty years of age.

Early in January he was laid in the vault in Holyrood, and on the same day, amid the " dool " for her father, his infant daughter was christened.

Beauty and charm were the heritage of this child of sorrow, but strife raged around her very cradle. An infant, helpless and fatherless, she was a valuable political asset. France and England were intriguing to gain possession of herself and her little barren, lawless country. At home the Earl of Arran and Cardinal Beaton perjured themselves for the post of power, and before she could leave her room, the Queen-Mother, Mary of Guise, lay distracted by the plots of the great nobles and dread lest the child might be taken from her and held in some strong castle during her minority.

Henry the Eighth's plan was to unite

STATE ENTRY OF QUEEN MARY INTO EDINBURGH
By William Hole, R.S.A.

Scotland to his own dominions by marrying the infant Queen to his son Edward, then a child of five years old; and the Queen-Mother's French relatives desired the alliance with Scotland in order to use the turbulent little country as a thorn in England's side. Henry sent an ambassador to demand that the child should be betrothed to the young Edward and handed over into his own keeping until she should be of marriageable age; and meanwhile the strongest fortresses in the country were to be delivered up to him by the Scots as an earnest of good faith.

The demands were too peremptory. The spirit of the nation revolted, and Mary of Guise's inclination was towards France and the ancient religion. For safety, the child was conveyed under a strong guard to Stirling Castle, then deemed impregnable. Natural defences were the steep rock and the winding river, and the Highlands were close by with wood and mountain in which to take refuge if special dan-

13

ger threatened. Lord Erskine, hereditary Keeper of the Castle, and her governors, the Lords Lindsay and Livingstone, were to guard the baby Queen against all enemies, Scot or foreigner, at the peril of their lives and goods.

In the church near the fortress the child was crowned at the age of nine months. The Queen-Mother, always striving to keep peace and win popularity in her adopted country, entertained the nobles to feasts and tournaments after the ceremony. When all was over, she " went on her feete to Our Lady of Lauriet [*i.e.* the shrine of the Virgin at Loretto in Musselburgh] praying for peace among her lordes and with the realm of England, and remained there twenty dayes in her prayers," Henry being engaged in preparations for carrying out his threat of invasion.

Winter passed in plots and threatening, then in spring the invading army landed at Leith. The instructions of the commander, the Earl of Hertford, were to

THE HOPE OF SCOTLAND

" burn and sack Edinburgh town, beat down and overthrow the Castle, sack Holyrood House and as many towns and villages about Edinburgh as you conveniently can ; sack and burn Leith, putting man, woman, and child to fire and sword without exception where any resistance shall be made against you. Then to Fife and do the same thing there, and thence to the Bishop's town of St. Andrews ; turn it upside down, spare no creature alive therein." Having crushed the country into a surly submission, they were to gain possession of the baby Queen and convey her into England.

Leith was burned and a " jolly fire " made at Holyrood ; but the Castle guns drove the English out of Edinburgh. They penetrated nearly as far as Stirling before they retired, devastating the country. In autumn they were upon the Borders again, and her watchful guardians carried the little Queen to Dunkeld, bringing her back when word came that the enemy had been

driven out. The abbeys of Kelso, Jedburgh, Melrose, and Dryburgh were burned; five market towns, forty-three villages, and sixteen fortified places destroyed, besides mills and hospitals, and the Borders laid waste.

During the years that the infant Queen lived in Stirling there took place the burning of George Wishart for heresy, the assassination in St. Andrews of her guardian, the Cardinal Beaton, and the siege of St. Andrews Castle. The castle fell, and among its defenders one John Knox, ex-priest and afterwards reformer, was sentenced to row for nineteen months in the French king's galleys.

After the battle of Pinkie, when the English army inflicted a calamitous defeat upon the Scots, the little girl was removed to the island of Inchmahone on the Lake of Monteith. Here she lived during the winter in the monastery guarded and taught by the prior, the monks, and her governors. Her nurse, Janet Sinclair, was

QUEEN MARY'S FIRST LEVEE
By William Hole, R.S.A.

with her, and her "four Maries," little
girls chosen from the noble families of
Scotland to be her companions—Mary
Beaton, Mary Seton, Mary Livingstone,
and Mary Fleming. "A goodlier child
was never seen, nor one more richly dowered by nature," and her beauty, grace, and
winsome ways were already passing into
a tradition.

Resistance toward England had deep-
ened into a passion of hatred ; the child's
guardians had appealed to France, and the
Hope of Scotland was to be betrothed to
the Dauphin and given into the care of
Henry II. Enemies to be avoided were the
English ships and the pirates with which
the seas at that time were swarming.
The King of France sent an army to expel
the Southrons, and Admiral Villegaignon
was entrusted with the task of bringing
home the child-Queen. The English being
on the alert on the seas between France
and Scotland, Villegaignon resolved to
carry her away from the west side, sailing

round the coast of Ireland. Accordingly, the galleys steered their course round the far north by the Orkney Islands, a voyage, according to the chronicler, which had never yet been made by galleys, because "they are not suitably built for resisting the violent onsets of that sea caused by the tides, which are there wonderfully strong, and by the perpetual storms."

At Dumbarton, where the royal child had waited five months in the fortress, the party was taken on board. With the Queen sailed her nurse and the four Maries; her three natural brothers, the Lord James, Prior of St. Andrews, Lord John, Prior of Coldingham, and Lord Robert, Prior of Holyrood House; the Lords Erskine and Livingstone, her guardians; Lady Fleming (a natural daughter of James IV. and extremely beautiful), the Prior of Inchmahone, and more than a hundred guards and servants.

The child about to make this adventurous journey was between five and six

years of age. While the vessel was still in the Clyde, messages were sent to the anxious mother.

" I assure you, Madame," wrote the Sieur de Brézé, Mary's new governor, " that the Queen, your daughter, fares as well and is as joyous as you have seen her for a long time."

The wind freshened as the ships approached the mouth of the estuary. "I desire to assure you, Madame, that in spite of the high winds of the last few days, which have tossed the ship very much, the Queen has never been sick, which makes me hope that she will suffer little in the open sea." When the voyage was over he wrote: "She has been less ill on the sea than any of her company, so that she made fun of those that were."

The child was safe in her mother's land, the Sieur de Villegaignon having steered his vessels past the English ships and other perils of the route.

" We were eighteen days upon the sea,"

wrote the Sieur de Brézé, giving a final account of the voyage, "with great tempests. Two or three times we were almost compelled to return to Dombertrand [Dumbarton], and one night when we were about ten leagues from the Cape of Cornwall the sea was wondrous stormy with the biggest waves I have seen in my life. The rudder of our galley broke, which threw us into great consternation, but our Lord was pleased to intervene so that we were able to replace the rudder almost at once in spite of the heavy sea that was running."

CHAPTER THE SECOND: THE HAPPY LAND OF FRANCE

CHAPTER THE SECOND
HAPPY LAND OF FRANCE

THE VOYAGERS HAD REACHED the coast of Brittany, and the spot where the child-Queen's foot first touched the soil of France was close by the village of Roscoff. Centuries later her descendant, Prince Charlie, a fugitive after the disaster of the Forty-Five, landed close by the little chapel which she caused to be built as a thankoffering for her successful voyage.

A few days later she was at Morlaix, where she was received by the Sieur de Rohan and the principal nobility of the country, and a solemn mass was sung in the church of Notre Dame.

On receiving the news of the child's safe arrival, her grandmother, Antoinette of Guise, wrote to the Queen-Dowager: "Madame, I felt happier than I can say when I heard that our little Queen had arrived in as good health as we could wish for her. I grieve for the anxiety which you must have felt during her voyage, and before you heard of her arrival here, and

23

alsofor the sorrow you must havefeltwhen she set out. . . .

" I will start this week, God willing, to meet her as quickly as I can, and bring her to St. Germains, according to the King's instructions."

At Orleans the Duchess met her grand-daughter, whom she describes in a letter to her son : "Sete petite dame. . . . She is very pretty indeed, and as intelligent a child as you could see. She is brune with a clear complexion, and I think she will be a beautiful girl, for her complexion is fine and clear, the skin white. The lower part of the face is very well formed ; the eyes are small and rather deep set, the face rather long. She is graceful and not shy, and on the whole we may be well content-ed with her."

The party proceeded by slow stages to St. Germains, Antoinette writing that " Our little Queen and all her train are as well as possible." The King announced her arrival in a letter to the Estates of

MARY BEATON

Scotland: " We have given orders that she shall be received, treated, and honoured in all our towns and other places through which she may pass as though she were our dearly loved consort the Queen in person, having power and right to grant pardons and set prisoners free. We have omitted nothing, we believe, of all the honours that should be paid to her, for we hold and esteem her for what she is, our daughter."

The faithful de Brézé wrote that the King had not yet seen her, " but he has set out from Moulins for that purpose." "Believe me, madame, he will not find her less charming and to his taste than all the others who have admired her beauty and intelligence."

Henry was anxious to meet her " since all who come here after seeing her praise her as a wonder. This increases my desire to see her, as I hope to do ere long." In November he was at St. Germains, and described her as "the most perfect child I have ever seen."

25

The beautiful little half-foreign girl had captivated the Court and all who met her. That "she governs the King and the Queen" was discovered not long after her arrival. Catherine de Medici wrote lovingly of "our little queenlet of Scotland," and she won the affection of the King's grave, middle-aged mistress, Diane de Poitiers, who has left a vivid description of her appearance and disposition. Among the many who welcomed the child on her arrival was her half-brother, the little Duc de Longueville, who wrote to his mother in Scotland that " he was resolved to do her all the service in his power."

Flattered and caressed, Mary was carefully brought up with her royal playmates, and her native grace and sweetness of disposition escaped spoiling by over-indulgence. Brantôme describes her eyes " beaming with life and intelligence, her appearance noble and full of charm." She became a wonder-child whose beauty and cleverness were noted in the Venetian

Minister's dispatches, and her fame spread as far as Sweden. Among the many contrasts in the little Queen's surroundings it is curious to find that Henry ii., an unfaithful husband, cruel at times in the government of his country, was a devoted father. Nothing which concerned the welfare of his children was too trivial, and he showed an especial tenderness for his little adopted daughter of Scotland, whose wit and brightness delighted him.

" The Scottish tongue," wrote Brantôme, " which is very rude and barbaric, she spoke so prettily that it sounded beautiful and pleasant in her although not in others. When she was dressed in the barbaric fashion of the savages of her country, her mortal form, in this coarse and rude dress, appeared that of a very goddess." She appears to have worn the Highland garb frequently when in the country, although appearing at Court with the other children in the stiff and quaint attire of the period.

27

MARY QUEEN OF SCOTS

A significant incident occurred at the festivities in connection with the wedding of Mary's uncle, the Duke of Guise, when the Scots Queen made what was probably her first appearance at Court. "I should like you to know, Madame, my good sister," the King wrote, "that I had invited to the wedding of my cousin . . . all the ambassadors of the various princes who are with me. He of England was not absent, and in his presence I took the opportunity of making my son the Dauphin dance with my daughter the Queen of Scotland. As he was talking with the Ambassador of the Emperor, my cousin the Cardinal of Guise approached, to whom I said that it was pretty to see them, and my cousin replied that it would be a charming marriage. The English Ambassador merely answered that he found much pleasure in watching them ; yet I am sure he found hardly any, and liked as little the caresses which he saw me give them." The grudge against the child had

CHAPTER THE THIRD
"A WONDER TO ALL TIME"

IN HAPPY IGNORANCE OF THE future the little companions grew up together, sharing their studies and recreations under the care of a host of governors and instructors. They learned Latin, modern languages, and history, and began to make some acquaintance with the works of contemporary authors. In singing Mary had the advantage of a naturally sweet voice with a lilt, and she was noted for the grace of her dancing.

The Dauphin, dowered with more spirit than strength, found his bent towards the outdoor and martial exercises in which his father excelled. At the age of six he wrote gleefully to the lieutenant of his company: "My King has told me that I shall follow him and serve him as soon as I am past seven." In thanking the warrior Duke of Guise for the present of a suit of armour, he wrote: "I am practising as often as I can in arms, so as to meet you as a gentle knight face to face, for I hope

33   c

that, with the favour of the lovely and virtuous lady your niece, half the honours of our fight will be mine."

The Queen of Scots was no whit behind her gallant little betrothed in her love of active pursuits. For outdoor amusements the children had horses, the two favourites of the little Queen being "La Bravane" and "Madame la Réale." They had dogs and falcons for hunting and hawking, and we find Mary writing to her mother in Scotland for "erth dogges" (terriers) and "petits hacquenais" (ponies) to give to the younger children.

About two years after Mary's arrival she was told that her mother was coming to visit the French Court.

"Madame," wrote the delighted child in announcing the news to her grandmother of Lorraine, "I have been very glad to be able to offer you these present lines, for the purpose of telling you the joyful news I have received from the Queen my mother, who has promised me, by her letter dated

April 23rd, that she will be here very soon
to see you and me, which will be to me the
greatest happiness I could desire in this
world. I am so glad about it that my only
thought now is to do my whole duty in all
things and to study to become very good,
in order to satisfy her wish to see me all
that you and she desire. I pray you, Madame, to increase my happiness by coming
hither soon if it is agreeable to you, and to
arm yourself with all the patience which
you know to be necessary in such a case as
this."

The Queen-Dowager arrived in due
course and received a royal welcome.
Nearly a year was spent at the Court and
with her kinsfolk of Lorraine, but the last
weeks of Mary's visit were shadowed by
the death of her son by her first marriage,
the little Duc de Longueville, and by still
sadder and more painful events.

A plot for the poisoning of the little
Queen came to light, and it was impossible
to discover who was involved and what

treachery might surround the child. The plan appears to have originated among the Scots in the Queen-Dowager's train and those in the French Court; but although one Robert Stewart, an archer of the guard, was arrested and put to torture as the ringleader, no admission could be drawn from him regarding his motives or accomplices nor the manner in which the scheme would be carried out. Whether Stewart was a madman inspired by some wild idea of his own, or whether this was one of the many plots of which the Queen of Scots was the centre throughout her lifetime, will never now be known; but the discovery must have filled the mother's mind with anxiety. Before she left France she appointed her brother the Cardinal of Lorraine as the little Queen's governor. For the next few years the child was withdrawn to some degree from the influence of Henry and Catherine and lived more under that of her grandmother and other relatives of the House of Guise.

" A WONDER TO ALL TIME "

" I have come to Meudon," she wrote to her mother when she was eleven, " to Madame my grandmother in order to keep the feast of Easter, because she and my uncle, Monsieur the Cardinal, wish that I should take the Sacrament, and I pray to God very humbly that I may make a good beginning."

Her studies were those of the learned women of the Renaissance. George Buchanan was her Latin master, and her literary tastes were fostered by the King's sister, Margaret of France, one of the most brilliant women of her time.

"Love learning, illustrious Prince," Mary wrote to her youthful betrothed, who was not fond of study. At the age of thirteen she delivered a Latin oration before the King, the Queen, and all the Court, her theme being that a knowledge of letters and the liberal arts was suitable and becoming for women.

Both in mind and character the Queen of Scots developed rapidly. Many of the distinguishing traits of her ancestors re-

vealed themselves. She loved music like her fathers, the kings of Scotland, and was a good performer on several instruments. She sang very well, Brantôme tells us, "attuning her voice to the lute, which she played very prettily with that fair white hand of hers and those well-shaped fingers, lovely as the fingers of Aurora." "Above all," he says, "she loved poetry and poets, but especially M. de Ronsard, M. de Bellay, and M. de Maison Fleur, who wrote charming poems and elegies for her," and the descendant of James I. of Scotland developed some poetic talent of her own, and wrote graceful verses which are commended by Brantôme.

"There is nothing," her uncle the Cardinal wrote to Mary of Guise, "which she hates so much as meanness"; and Sir James Melville wrote that "she was naturally liberall, mair than she had moyen." Being absolutely without fear, she was an intrepid huntress. Her courage commended her to her uncle Francis, Duke of

Guise, the great warrior who stole back Calais from the English. " Niece," he said to her upon one occasion, " there is one trait in which, more than in all others, I recognise my own blood in you : you are as brave as any of my men-at-arms. If women went into battle now as they did in ancient times, I think you would know how to die well."

The Cardinal wrote urging Mary of Guise to visit his royal pupil once more ; but the Queen-Dowager, almost sinking under the cares of the kingdom which she was trying to govern for her daughter, never again saw the child who had become a proverb throughout Europe for her beauty, grace, and the promise of her mind and character.

KNOX PREACHING BEFORE THE LORDS OF CONGREGATION
By Sir David Wilkie, R.S.A.

CHAPTER THE FOURTH
"I WAS THE QUEEN O'
BONIE FRANCE"

CHAPTER THE FOURTH
"QUEEN O' BONIE FRANCE"

STRANGE ALTHOUGH IT MAY AP-
pear, no perversity of opposition was a-
roused in the two children whom policy
and state-craft had destined for each other.
The affection between the gentle, delicate
boy and the brilliant girl seems to have
grown with their growth. "The Dauphin
is very fond of the little Queen of Scotland,"
the Venetian Ambassador wrote in 1555 ;
"she is a very pretty little girl of twelve or
thirteen. Sometimes one sees them caress
each other, retiring all by themselves into
a corner of the room so that no one can
hear their little secrets."

Three years later, when Mary was fif-
teen, the Dauphin being a little more than
a year younger, state-craft dictated that
the marriage should take place. On 19th
April 1558 the youthful pair plighted their
troth before the Cardinal of Lorraine in
the great hall of the Louvre, and on the
following Sunday the wedding was held
with extraordinary magnificence. Noth-

43

ing was omitted which could emphasise the importance which Henry placed upon the Scottish alliance. All Paris rejoiced when the bridal procession passed on the way to the cathedral of Notre Dame, Mary being escorted by the King and the Duke of Lorraine. Her dress was of pure white, and she glittered with jewels.

" From her neck hung a pendant of inestimable value, with a jewelled collar, precious stones, and other riches of great price," says an old chronicler who seems to have come out of the *Arabian Nights*. " On her head she wore a crown of gold ornamented with pearls, diamonds, rubies, sapphires, emeralds, and other stones of inestimable value, and from the centre of the said crown there hung a carbuncle estimated to be worth five hundred thousand dollars or more."

Following the bride came Catherine de Medici, the Queen of Navarre, and the King's sister, Margaret of France ; while the Dauphin was escorted by the King of

Navarre.   After the ceremony Mary sal-
uted her husband by the title of King of
Scotland, and pageants and a ball brought
to a close a day which seemed to promise
renewed glory to France.

" All things smiled beneath the rays of
that dawn, and it seemed as though happiness must pour forth her favours with
full hands upon a marriage whose knot
had been tied in heaven, in order to win
the approval of all the earth."

But side by side with all this splendour
other forces were working, of circumstances apparently too trivial to be feared, and
character too insignificant to be heeded at
the time ; shaping the young Queen's destiny.

The absence of Mary of Guise signified
disorder and rebellion in the little country
which was her daughter's dowry. Among
the nine Scottish envoys who represented
her were the Lord James, Mary's half-
brother, the silent, ambitious man, disap-
pointed from birth, who had been reminded

in early youth that only a "squalling girl" stood between him and the throne of Scotland. If he could not wear a crown he would at least wield power.

George Buchanan, Mary's Latin tutor, who composed an enthusiastic ode upon her marriage, was in after years to blacken his pupil's memory in his *Detectio*. The sad, ambitious Catherine de Medici, who passed through the streets on the wedding day seated side by side with the Queen-Dauphiness, changed gradually from love to cold dislike as the influence of the Guises prevailed with her daughter-in-law. And all unthinkingly Henry II. fixed irrevocably the destiny of his son's wife when, on the death of Mary I. of England, he caused her to assume the title and arms of Queen of Scotland, England, and Ireland. From that time she was regarded as the enemy of Elizabeth and the Protestant cause in England, and her indignant foes only a-waited the opportunity to throw her in the dust.

"QUEEN O' BONIE FRANCE"

After the wedding the young Dauphin and his wife loved each other, and life went on happily for them save for the frequent illnesses of Francis. The beautiful Queen of Scots was more admired than ever at pageants and Court ceremonies, and the youthful pair spent much of their leisure in the country châteaux of Henry and the nobles of the realm.

In June 1559 preparations were made for a double wedding in the Royal House of France. The King's sister, Margaret, " La bonté du monde," was to marry the Duke of Savoy at the same time that Mary's friend and playfellow, the youthful Princess Elizabeth, became the third wife of King Philip of Spain. The history of these times was only in the making, and no one seems to have shuddered when it became known that the Duke of Alva, a name now synonymous with callous oppression, was to be Philip's proxy at the latter ill-fated wedding. A three days' tournament was proclaimed, and, triumphant

47

in the success of two powerful alliances, Henry caused the Queen-Dauphiness to be preceded to the lists by heralds shouting, "Place, place, pour la reine d'Angleterre!" an insult never forgotten nor forgiven by Elizabeth.

On the third day of the tournament, when the sports were almost over, Henry suddenly surprised every one by challenging the Comte de Montgomery to break a lance with him. The Comte was unwilling, and Queen Catherine, who had been troubled by dreams of coming misfortune, begged the King to desist; but Henry remained inflexible. The two combatants met, and in the shock his adversary's lance was broken, a splinter entering the King's right eye. Henry was carried from the lists a dying man, and the rejoicing was changed into mourning. Ten days later a boy and girl found themselves King and Queen of France.

Mary's position was now perhaps the most brilliant in the world : Queen-Con-

HENRY, LORD DARNLEY

sort of France, and Queen in her own right;
envied by all those who had seen the success of the late King's ambitious schemes.
But the foundations of her splendour were
insecure. The boy-King was far too
young and delicate to govern, and under
the reign of the Guises religious and political strife convulsed the land. Ill news
came from the Queen-Mother, alone in
troubled splendour as Regent of Scotland.
Calvinism, treated in France as a moral
poison, was gaining the mastery in the
northern country, and the Queen's health
and position were in danger among the
rebellious nobles.

A terrible rumour went abroad regarding the young King. It was reported that
he had become afflicted with leprosy, which
was only to be cured by bathing in the blood
of young children. "Monster, give us back
our children!" the peasants cried when
they met him in the forests. The tumult of
Amboise broke out among the Huguenots.
The plot was suppressed, and the summer

D

of 1559 darkened by the execution and tortures of the unfortunate conspirators.

Anxious letters passed between Mary and her mother. The storm in Scotland burst in 1560, when the opposing party triumphed and Mary of Guise took refuge in Edinburgh Castle. Worn out with care and strife, the harassed, courageous soul passed away soon afterwards at the age of forty-five.

Grave responsibilities had fallen upon the young Queen of France and Scotland. "While she lived," Mary said after her mother's death, "I was less troubled with the care of that country, and now I must be troubled with the care of it myself." In November 1560 the King's health was giving rise to the gloomiest forebodings. The prophecies of the astrologers were recalled, foretelling that Francis would not live longer than eighteen years, and Mary, with the Queen-Mother and the young princes, took part in processions to the churches to pray for his recovery.

A swelling developed behind the right

50

ear, and the boy was doomed. On the 5th December he passed away. The Court hastened to congratulate the new King his brother, and the life which had flickered out soon ceased to be remembered. "By degrees every one is forgetting the death of the late King," wrote the Venetian Ambassador, " except the little Queen, his widow, who, being no less noble-minded than beautiful and graceful, the thoughts of widowhood at so early an age and the loss of a consort who was so great a King and so dearly loved her . . . so afflict her that she will not receive any consolation, but brooding over her disaster with passionate and doleful lamentations, she universally inspires great pity."

In after years the young King, Charles ix., held his brother fortunate. "Ah, Francis, happy brother," he would exclaim, looking at Mary's portrait, " though your life and reign were short, yet were you to be envied in this that you were the possessor of that angel and the object of her love."

51

CHAPTER THE FIFTH: "L'ON VOIT SOUS BLANC ATOUR"

"SOUS BLANC ATOUR"

THE BRIEF ELUSIVE SPELL OF happiness was over. In her "sad and plaintive song," the lament which she composed for her young husband, Mary deplored her early widowhood. At eighteen the part for which she had been carefully trained was hers no longer, and a new, unknown life lay before her.

Feeling the antagonism of Catherine de Medici, "La Royne Marye" retired from the Court, spending some months with her beloved grandmother and other relatives in the provinces. Her desire would have been to live "a simple dowager" in France, but the indifference of the new Regent and the wishes of her own subjects soon showed that her home must be in her own little distant heritage. After a visit from her brother, the Lord James, she began to prepare for her return to *la lourde Écosse*, a country at that time reported the most lawless in Europe, where Protestant was at feud with Catholic, Saxon with Celt, Borderer with Lowlander,

and where few men, save their kings, had as yet learned to be chivalrous.

To her brother, who had long since exchanged the character of a Catholic prior for that of a fervent Protestant, she announced her decision to return to Edinburgh instead of casting in her lot with the Catholics of the North.

" I will be plain with you," she said to the English Ambassador, Throgmorton, " and tell you what I would all the world should think of me. The religion which I profess I take to be the most acceptable to God ; and, indeed, neither do I know, nor desire to know, any other. . . . I have been brought up in this religion, and who might credit me in anything if I might show myself light in this case ? " In reply to the Ambassador's arguments she said : " You may perceive that I am none of those that will change my religion every year ; . . . I mean to constrain none of my subjects, and I trust they shall have no support to constrain me."

56

THE MURDER OF RIZZIO
By David Scott, R.S.A.

"SOUS   BLANC   ATOUR"

An envoy had been sent to demand a
safe-conduct from Elizabeth for Mary—
the first opportunity afforded the English
Queen for humiliating her rival. Elizabeth's reply was a curt refusal, and to
Throgmorton Mary expressed her disappointment in terms at once pathetic and
dignified. The refusal of a safe-conduct,
she said, showed that Elizabeth believed
her to be a woman without friends. With
regard to his mistress's complaint that
Mary had refused to ratify the Treaty of
Edinburgh, that document having been
drawn up without the consent of herself
or her husband, she could take no steps
regarding it without first consulting the
nobles of Scotland.

Throgmorton reminded her that she had
adopted the arms of England.

"Mr. Ambassador," replied Mary, "I
was then under the commandment of
King Henry my father, and of the King
my lord and husband." Since their deaths,
she added, as the Ambassador was well

aware, she had neither borne the arms nor used the title of England. She hoped that the winds might prove favourable, that she might not fall into the power of the English Queen. "And if," Mary continued, "she be so hard-hearted as to desire my end, she may then do her pleasure. Peradventure that might be better than for me to live. God's will be done."

Throgmorton, whom Sir Henry Wotton had characterised as "an honest man sent to lie abroad for the good of his country," was deeply impressed with this interview. Like so many others who have recorded their impressions of the Queen of Scots, he was compelled to admire the woman even while seeing in her an enemy to his country.

At last all was ready, and at St. Germains the final farewells were made to Queen Catherine, the young King, and the Duke of Anjou, who had accompanied Mary from Paris, attended by a train of nobles. A week later Throgmorton was able to write to Elizabeth that in Calais his

servant had seen the Queen of Scots " haling out of that haven on the 14th inst. about noon, with two galleys and two great ships."

Among those who accompanied " La Royne blanche " to her Scottish home were three of her uncles, Claude, Duke of Aumale; Francis, the Grand Prior; and René, Marquis d'Elbœuf; her four Maries, who reappear in the light of history on the deck of the Queen's galley; and Brantôme the historian. "As she was leaving the port," says the latter, "she saw a vessel wrecked in front of her and most of the mariners perish, not having studied the current or the depth; and at the sight she cried, 'Oh God! what omen of voyage is this?'"

The wind rose, and the vessel entered the open sea. The Queen of Scots, says Brantôme, went to the stern, leaning both arms upon the taffrail, and shedding many tears as she looked back to the place she was leaving. "Farewell, France," she sighed; and she remained there until it began

59

to grow dark. "Night spreads her black veil before my eyes," she said, "to prevent me from seeing France." A bed was made for her on the deck, and she gave orders that she should be awakened at dawn if any part of France were still in view. At daybreak, the wind having fallen, land was still in sight, and she rose and looked her last upon France.

The sailors plied the oars, and the land receded. " Farewell, dear France," said Mary ; "farewell, dear France. It is over. I shall never see thee more ! "

Regretting as much as she was regretted, she was leaving behind her the only place of peace and security that she was ever to know. In France, through all the strife and misgovernment of the two last reigns, Mary Stewart had been beloved and idolised. "If the silver moon," wrote some gallant chronicler, describing Mary's appearance at a Court ceremony, " had appeared shining in the midst of her stars, her lustre would have been dimmed beside

such rare perfections and such dazzling loveliness."

In her adopted country Mary bore a spotless reputation and is remembered with pity and affection. Speaking in Edinburgh a few years ago, an Ambassador of France reminded us that " she was not only one of our queens, but also one of our poets, and in the country districts of France women of the people still sing their children to sleep with the old ballads of Queen Mary Stewart."

CHAPTER   THE SIXTH
"HER NORTHERN DOOM"

QUEEN MARY IN EDINBURGH AFTER CARBERRY

By James Drummond, R.S.A.

CHAPTER THE SIXTH
"HER NORTHERN DOOM"

THE LAND TO WHICH MARY WAS returning had become no more easy to govern since the body of the Queen-Regent had been refused Christian burial in its soil. The Protestants, cruelly oppressed in France, held the mastery in the country which the widow of a French king was to govern. The beautiful cathedrals and churches of her religion had been desecrated and lay in ruins. Art and letters were neglected, and public and private quarrels kept the country in a state almost of anarchy.

Besides heresy, witchcraft was rife in the Queen's barren and lawless heritage. Napier of Merchiston, one of the few enlightened individuals of the country, practised necromancy in his castle near Edinburgh. The gaunt, ferocious Lord Ruthven was reported to be a wizard. Highborn ladies were suspected of being in league with the Evil One, and there was hardly a town or a village in Scotland

E

without its old crone who was credited with a mysterious alliance with the powers of darkness.

The Highlands were an almost unknown and unexplored country, whose inhabitants differed in race, language, and customs from the southern part of the kingdom. The Borderers were at perpetual feud with the English, with their Lowland neighbours, and with each other. The comparatively civilised middle region was peopled by a race the most " dour " in Europe—burghers and peasants of independent character, intensely earnest and ready to defy king or bishop, or the allied powers of Europe. With the nobles the Queen-Mother's regency had been one long conflict, and the man who swayed men's minds in Scotland was John Knox, once a galley-slave, and now the leader of the Protestant party in Scotland.

As little as her fathers did Mary allow herself to be daunted by the almost hopeless task she was undertaking. By the

time her little fleet cast anchor in Leith
roads her naturally high spirits had risen,
and when the English Ambassador came
on board her galley, one of the first to pay
his respects to the young Queen, the gra-
ciousness of her reception of him, and her
beauty, completely disarmed the schem-
ing Randolph. The minister of Elizabeth
in Scotland, it was his duty, as he con-
ceived it, to involve this young girl in
trouble for the good of his own country,
yet he was captivated against his will, and
wrote to his mistress a description of her
rival which must have caused that jealous
lady many a pang.

The arrival of the ships having taken
the authorities by surprise, Mary and her
suite had to make their way to Holyrood
mounted " on the miserable hackneys of
the country," says Brantôme, "with har-
ness to match." On the way she was met
by some artisans who had broken prison,
where they had been confined for the dire
offence of celebrating a masque of Robin

Hood on May Day, which that year had chanced to fall upon a Sunday. The Queen pardoned the revellers, winning for herself the goodwill of the populace, but the condemnation of John Knox, who attributed this act of clemency on Mary's part to her having been " sufficiently instructed that all they did was done in despite of religion."

Among the masques which greeted the formal entry of the young Queen into the city were references to her " idolatry," which she apparently thought it wise to ignore. It had been proposed to burn a priest in effigy, but this was abandoned, although some children, in presenting the Queen with a Bible, "made some speech regarding the putting away of the mass." Mary's lovely face and her charm of manner were making a conquest of her subjects, and all went well until Sunday, when mass was celebrated in the Queen's private chapel in Holyrood.

To a recently converted people this was

an abomination. In grief and anger, and
crying out that " the idolatrous priest
must die the death," the Master of Lindsay and other zealots ran to the chapel.
Lord James held the door while the service was proceeding, and it is probable that
the Queen was undisturbed by the brawl
outside. A rush was made upon the priest
as he was leaving Holyrood, but the
Queen's half-brothers, the Lords Robert
and John, conveyed him to his lodgings,
and " the godly departed with great grief
of heart."

On the following Sunday John Knox
preached a terrible sermon against the
mass, and Mary, probably expecting that
the Reformer might be as amenable to her
charm as her other subjects, summoned
him to her presence.

Intrepidly meeting his severe look, she
firmly but courteously inquired why he had
instigated her subjects to rebel against
her.

Knox replied that he had obeyed the

voice of God by denouncing idolatry. Mary inquired whether he thought she had no just authority, and quoted his book, the *First Blast of the Trumpet against the Monstrous Regiment of Women.*

Knox compared himself with Plato, and his book with that philosopher's *Republic.* With regard to the authority of the Queen, "If," he said, "the realm finds no inconvenience from the regiment of a woman, that which they approve of I shall not further disallow than within my own breast, but shall be as well content to live under your Grace as Paul was to live under Nero."

Restraining her feelings, Mary said the Reformer taught subjects to adopt a faith not permitted by their princes. Were subjects, she inquired, not to obey their rulers?

"True religion," replied Knox, "was of God; the Israelites were not of the religion of Pharaoh, nor the early Christians of that of Nero."

"But none of these," objected Mary, "raised the sword against their princes."

"God, Madam," rejoined Knox, "had not given them the power nor the means." He went on to explain that a father being struck by frenzy, his children might bind his hands. "Even so, Madam, is it with princes that would murder the children of God that are subject to them."

"I perceive," said Mary, "that my subjects must obey you and not me."

"Both," answered John Knox, "should be subject to God and His troubled Church."

On Mary's alluding to her conscience:—

"Conscience, Madam," he cried; "conscience requireth knowledge, and I fear me that of right knowledge ye have none. Have you heard any truth but such as the Pope and the Cardinals have allowed?"

"You interpret the Scriptures one way," said the Queen, "and they in another; whom shall I believe, and who shall be judge?"

When he quoted the Confession of Faith, she said he was too hard for her, "but if

71

they were here that she had heard, they would answer him."

Knox asserted his readiness to meet and argue with the most learned Papist in Europe and demonstrate the utter vanity and falsehood of the Romish faith; upon which the interview closed.

Mary's gay spirit was not quenched by the difficulties of her position. She found pleasure in hunting and hawking on the large tracts of waste land in her new kingdom. Often she would leave the ladies of her train far behind while she urged her horse after some quarry. She practised archery and played golf, retiring to St. Andrews or Burntisland for these recreations, and "living like a *bourgeoise* wife with my little family." She is reported to have worn men's clothing and mixed with the people at country fairs and in Edinburgh, as her father James v. had done before her. In her little Court she entertained her nobles and friends, and " in fences, in masking, and other prodigalities, fain

JAMES HEPBURN, EARL OF BOTHWELL

would fools have counterfeited France," as her critics observed with insular contempt for customs differing from their own.

With a certain amount of suspicion, due to her religion and her foreign ways, the Queen was winning popularity among her subjects, and her confiding attitude disarmed opposition and made the treacherous seem true until the test came. Among those who danced pavanes and galliards in Holyrood were the weak, unstable Arran, who went mad for love of the Queen, and Argyll, one of the leaders of the Congregation. Married to the Queen's half-sister and friend, the lovely daughter of James v., his position in these troubled times was one of some difficulty, and his changes of attitude capable of explanation.

The keen-faced, courtly Maitland of Lethington, Secretary of State, was another : " the flower of the wits of Scotland; " Michael Wylie (Machiavelli) as his countrymen called him. Well did he merit the term ; he was true only to one prin-

ciple, the union of Scotland with England. To secure this, he maintained, would bring as much honour as was won by the men who fought beside Bruce for freedom; and the end justified the means. He ridiculed John Knox in the very face of the Reformer, whose sledge-hammer arguments were no weapon against the nimble rapier-thrusts of the Secretary's wit, and was regarded by him with horror as a man professing no religion, either Catholic or Protestant. A little over forty when he first met her, Maitland fell violently in love with Mary Fleming, the most beautiful of the four Maries and the favourite of her mistress; and this passion proving stronger than the other, he was faithful for a time to the Queen.

Maitland's rival in diplomacy was Randolph, the English Ambassador. Continually foiled by the Scot, he congratulated himself when he saw where his adversary's affections lay, that the Secretary would now, " wise as he is, show himself a

fool." One of the first to fall under the spell of the young Queen, he yet faithfully pursued his design for her undoing, and he was so little romantic in his passion for Mary Beaton as to turn it to account in drawing from her information regarding her mistress, which was duly forwarded to Elizabeth.

Of the men of letters who had followed Mary from the Court of France, Brantôme returned early to his own country and lived to commemorate her story. Chastelard, poet and musician, a nephew of Bayard, the "chevalier sans peur et sans reproche," lingered to his own undoing and died a shameful death.

Bothwell, the rake; boastful, quarrelsome, unscrupulous, yet the one man in Scotland who had consistently remained true to the Queen-Dowager, made a bad beginning with her daughter. A brawl in the streets first roused her ire against him, and she banished him from Edinburgh. Not long afterwards the Earl of Arran

came to her with the penitent confession of a plot said to have been contrived by himself and Bothwell, to murder the Lord James and seize upon the Government. It soon became evident that Arran was insane and the plot a delusion, yet a suspicion seems to have lingered in the Queen's mind regarding Bothwell, who took refuge in his castle of the Hermitage near Jedburgh, and wrote letters declaring his innocence and expressing his loyalty to his sovereign.

But Mary's prejudice was not to be so readily overcome. "Anything he can say or do," wrote the English Ambassador, "can little prevail. Her purpose is to put him out of the country;" and, in effect, Bothwell soon sailed for France, where he became Captain of the Scottish Guard.

Already he had been a page, a Border raider, a lieutenant-general in the service of Mary of Guise, and an envoy to France. He was reported to have studied the Black Art, and he had won the hearts of many

women who had cause to lament his un-
faithfulness. A man with such a character
was bound to go far ; yet at the time of his
exile few would have foretold how strange
a career would be his, nor how fatally his
destiny would become involved with
that of the Queen.

CHAPTER THE SEVENTH: A YOUNG PRINCE CHARMING

THE ABDICATION OF MARY QUEEN OF SCOTS
By Sir William Allan, P.R.S.A.

CHAPTER THE SEVENTH
YOUNG PRINCE CHARMING

MARY'S PRINCIPAL ADVISER AF-
ter her return to Scotland was the Lord
James, whom she created Earl of Mar, and
one of her first public actions was to issue
a proclamation declaring that she would
not interfere with her subjects' religion.

Trying to cultivate friendly relations
with England, she accepted Elizabeth's
assurance that the ships of war which had
hovered around her little fleet on the way
home had been merely on the watch for
pirates, and replied in cordial terms to the
English Queen's congratulations upon her
successful voyage.

In the autumn after her arrival she set
out upon a progress through her northern
dominions, and found the Earl of Huntly
and his clan in rebellion. The most powerful of the Catholic nobles, Huntly had been
at the head of those who had sent an em-
bassy to France urging Mary to land in the
Highlands, which were still for the most
part of her own religion.

81   F

The consequence would probably have been civil war, but a certain resentment seems to have lingered in Huntly's mind against the Lord James, whose counsel had prevailed with the Queen. In the summer following Mary's return, Sir John Gordon, a son of Huntly's, having attacked and wounded Lord Ogilvie in the streets of Edinburgh, was committed to prison. Escaping soon afterwards, he fled to Aberdeenshire, and, dreading the Queen's vengeance, roused his father's clan. On reaching Inverness, Mary demanded the surrender of the castle, which was held by some of Huntly's retainers. The defenders capitulated, but Mary refused to visit the Earl, who had sent to protest his loyalty. Deeply offended, Huntly assembled his followers, and was reported to be lying in wait for Mary at the passage of the Spey. The Queen's spirit always rose in the presence of danger, and she advanced fearlessly. "The weather was extreame fowle and cold," according to Randolph, an un-

willing member of the expedition, "yet I never saw her merrier, never dismayed." She was heard to declare that she only wished she was a man, " to know what life it was to lie all night in the fields, or to walk on the causeway with a jack and knapschalle [steel headpiece], a Glasgow buckler, and a broadsword at her side." Upon her brother she bestowed the lands and earldom of Moray, and threatened Huntly with outlawry if he did not surrender.

At Corrichie the Gordons encountered Mary's forces under the Earl of Moray. The clansmen were defeated, and Huntly fell dead from his horse. Moray compelled his sister to be present at the execution of Sir John Gordon at Aberdeen, and the Queen fainted at the sight. Her desire for vengeance was more than gratified; she pardoned Huntly's two remaining sons, and took his daughter, the Lady Jean Gordon, under her own protection.

Her first parliament was opened in per-

son by the Queen, who made a little speech in her pretty foreign-sounding Scots. Wearing her royal robes, and accompanied by her ministers, her four Maries, and the ladies of her Court, she returned to Holyrood by way of the High Street and the Canongate. The smiles and blessings of the people followed the little procession, while John Knox, looking gloomily from his window, could see nothing save the " targetted tails and styncken pride of women."

The preachers still remained insensible to the charm of the Queen, whom they publicly denounced as an idolatress. " They pray," said Randolph, "that God will either turn her heart or send her a short life. Of what spirit or charity this proceedeth I leave to be discussed by the great divines." When Mary gave a ball in Holyrood, John Knox characterised the dignified, stately dances of the age as "a skipping not very meet for honest women."

Time went on, and various projects had been made for the re-marriage of the

YOUNG PRINCE CHARMING

Queen of Scots. The Kings of Sweden and Denmark, the Prince of Orange, the Archduke Charles, Don Carlos of Spain, and the Duke of Anjou were among her suitors; but in view of the succession, it was desirable to win the approval of Elizabeth. Being consulted with regard to a fitting match for her cousin, the English Queen, after many preliminaries, suggested—the Earl of Leicester !

" Is that," asked Mary, " in conformity with her promise to use me as a sister or a daughter ? " and she became ill with vexation. John Knox was unable to refrain from the subject in the pulpit, and being summoned to answer for a vehement sermon regarding her marriage, reduced the Queen to indignant tears.

Meanwhile the young Henry Darnley, " un bien beaul jeusne homme," Mary's cousin, came from England, with his father, the banished Earl of Lennox. He was openly a suitor for the hand of the Queen, and it was hinted that the match

would not be unacceptable to Elizabeth. Darnley was three years younger than Mary ; of undeveloped character, weak and unstable, as his after conduct proved him to be, but trained in all the accomplishments of the time, and possessing the charm of the Stewarts. With such a prize in view, he exercised all his most winning qualities, and " his courteous dealing with all men was well spoken of."

During some weeks of stormy weather the young people were thrown much into one another's society ; then Mary nursed her cousin through an attack of measles, and the result was, if not that Darnley fell in love with the Queen, Mary lost her heart to the " lady-faced " youth. A betrothal took place privately in Stirling Castle in the room of Mary's Italian Secretary, Riccio, and the pair being within the forbidden degree, messages were sent asking for the Pope's dispensation for their marriage.

But Mary was not yet free from thwart-

ing and vexation. No sooner did Elizabeth receive tidings that a marriage was likely to take place between her young rival and Darnley than she announced that such an alliance was " directly prejudicial to the sincere amity between both the queens, and consequently perilous to the peace of both realms." She demanded the immediate return of father and son, and imprisoned the Countess of Lennox in the Tower.

The Protestants opposed the match on the ground that the young man was a Catholic.

Already Darnley had offended the Earl of Moray, and neither he nor Argyll appeared at the convention summoned by Mary at Perth for the announcement of her marriage. Before leaving the town Mary received intelligence that her chief minister and her brother-in-law had conspired together to seize Darnley and herself on their way to Edinburgh.

The Queen was in no mood for further

trifling. Travelling at full speed, she escaped the combined forces of her brother and Argyll. Arriving in Edinburgh, she summoned Moray to appear before her, and on his refusal called her vassals to arms. A few days later the marriage took place at Holyrood, and Mary bestowed upon her husband the title of King of Scotland. The capital rejoiced, but Moray's friends were rising on every side. Argyll was active in the West Highlands ; Glencairn and Ochiltree, the Earl of Rothes, Lord Boyd, and Kirkcaldy of Grange were with the insurgents. With pistols at her side, and accompanied by her husband and his father, the Earl of Lennox, Mary placed herself at the head of her troops and rode in pursuit of the rebels. At Glasgow they evaded her, but made a dash upon Edinburgh, where the inhabitants refused to rise. Retreating hastily to the south, they were followed by Mary. Some dispersed, and others were chased over the Borders into England.

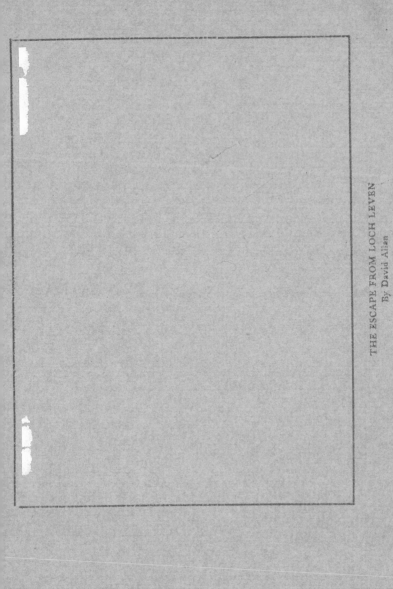

THE ESCAPE FROM LOCH LEVEN
By David Allan

YOUNG PRINCE CHARMING

So ended the Run-about-Raid, and Elizabeth, who had secretly aided Moray with troops and gold, sent for him to London and in presence of the French and Spanish Ambassadors forced him to declare that she was entirely innocent of encouraging him in his "abominable treason."

CHAPTER THE EIGHTH
GATHERING CLOUDS

CHAPTER THE EIGHTH
GATHERING CLOUDS

MARY'S HASTY AND IMPRUDENT marriage was followed by almost as speedy disappointment. Within a few weeks of the wedding, Darnley's arrogance had offended the nobles, and it became evident that his wooing of the Queen had been prompted only by ambition.

" To all honest men he is intolerable," reported the English Ambassador, " and almost forgetful of her already, that hath adventured so much for his sake. What shall become of her, or what life with him she shall lead, that already taketh so much upon him as to control and command her, I leave it to others to think." Even more significant is Randolph's statement that " he is counted proud, disdainful, and suspicious, which kind of men this soil, of any other, can worse bear."

Within a few months of his marriage he had become associated with a band of young men as wild and irresponsible as himself, neglecting his wife and passing

93

" his time in hunting and hawking, and such other pleasures as were agreeable to his appetite." To other faults he added that of intemperance. Drinking heavily one day with his companions at a banquet, the Queen implored him to desist, when he replied to her in terms so insulting that she withdrew in tears.

The Earl of Moray being in exile, and so many of her lords in disgrace, Mary was led to depend upon a new set of supporters. During the late rebellion the Earl of Bothwell, "the stoutest but worst thought of" upholder of the Kirk, had been allowed to return to Scotland and establish himself in his Border estates. About the same time Lord Gordon, son of the Earl of Huntly, obtained his freedom and was restored to his father's lands and title.

These two noblemen attaching themselves to the Queen's party, Mary placed confidence in them as others failed. Bothwell was reinstated as Warden of the Borders, and his marriage with Huntly's sis-

ter, Lady Jean Gordon, took place in Holyrood, the Queen entertaining the guests with royal generosity.

The young King's desire for power being greater than his capacity for business, Mary had to depend upon the services of her Italian secretary Riccio for carrying on public affairs. This man, a native of Piedmont, spoke French as well as Italian, and finding that her French secretaries betrayed her secrets to Catherine de Medici, the Queen had employed him in her foreign correspondence. He proved capable and discreet, and was consulted by his mistress upon important matters. The secretary was small and ill-favoured, but "a merry fellow," according to Melville. Gifted with a beautiful voice, he was an accomplished musician as well as a man of education, and the nobles were not slow in resenting the favour shown him by his royal mistress.

"If," wrote Mary, in a private memorandum, "the sovereign finds a man of humble

condition, and poor in worldly goods, but of a generous and faithful heart, and capable of serving the state, must he be debarred from all advancement?" She found herself in the position of her ancestors who employed what their subjects contemptuously termed " masons " and " fiddlers " of foreign birth because none of their own countrymen were capable of doing the work.

On Darnley's first coming to Scotland, both father and son had paid court to Riccio in the hope of gaining the Italian's influence in furthering the match. Darnley admitted the secretary to some degree of intimacy, playing tennis and fishing with him. After the marriage, not being content with the title of King, he demanded the crown matrimonial, which secured to him equal rights with his consort and the sole sovereignty in the case of her death. But by this time his weakness and incapacity were fully proved. Mary declined to admit him to power, and Darnley discov-

MAITLAND OF LETHINGTON

ered that she had been supported in her refusal by the secretary.

The slight to his self-esteem made Darnley the mortal enemy of Riccio. With the Queen he was deeply offended, and the malcontents and plotters, of whom there were only too many around Mary Stewart, saw in the moody, discontented lad a fitting tool for their purpose.

The nobles who had risen to oppose the marriage were waiting for revenge. Lethington and the Earl of Morton, Chancellor of the Kingdom, secretly in league with the banished lords, worked upon the jealous, shallow mind of Darnley to form a plot with the men who had taken up arms against him. Lord Ruthven, admitted to their counsels, caused Darnley to swear that he would conceal any enterprise in which they might embark from the Queen, and made it a condition that " the lords banished for the Word of God might return to their country and estates." Soon afterwards the Earl of Lennox was in Eng-

97   G

land bearing to the rebel lords a document
by which his son bound himself to obtain
their pardon " as soon as by their help
and supply he obtained the crown-matri-
monial." In return Moray and his supporters agreed to maintain Darnley " in his
just title to the Crown of Scotland, failing
of succession to our sovereign lady.

" And if any manner of persons will
usurp or gainsay the said just title, the
said lords shall maintain, defend, and set
forward the same as best shall please the
said noble prince, without fear of life or
death, and shall seek and pursue them that
usurp as shall please the said noble prince
to command, to extirpate them out of the
realm of Scotland, or take or slay them."

Darnley was actually inexperienced enough to believe in the sincerity of this engagement with his own enemies.

No suspicion seems to have entered the
mind of Mary, but the plot was not unknown outside the palace. On the 13th of
February 1566, Randolph had written to the

Earl of Leicester : " I know that there are practices in hand, contrived between the father and son, to come to the crown against her will. I know that if that take effect which is intended, David, with the consent of the King, shall have his throat cut within these ten days. Many things grievouser and worse than this are brought to my ears ; yea, of things intended against her own person, which, because I think better to keep secret than to write to Mr. Secretary, I speak of them but now to your lordship."

Nearly a month elapsed between the writing of this letter and the carrying out of the plot, yet neither Randolph nor Leicester found time to send a word of warning to the intended victim.

Having instilled into the mind of her husband dark suspicions of the honour of the Queen, it was agreed that Riccio should be slain in the presence of his mistress. Mary, who was then within three months of her confinement, would prob-

99

ably not survive the shock ; in any case, she would be disgraced and discredited, and her rebellious subjects would have a pretext for deposing her. Darnley's destruction after that was easy ; an object of hatred and contempt to all sections of the people, his own folly would hasten his ruin, and the conspirators would gain supreme power in Scotland.

On Sunday the 3rd of March began the national fast in Edinburgh, and the pulpits of Knox, Craig, and the more zealous of the Calvinistic divines rang with denunciations of anti-Christ and calls to vengeance upon the enemies of God. The town was full of religious fanatics, and the banished lords were returning secretly to Scotland.

CHAPTER THE NINTH

THE STORM BURSTS

CHAPTER THE NINTH
THE STORM BURSTS

IT WAS IN VAIN THAT MARY EN-
treated her husband to accompany her to
the opening of Parliament. The lad replied in surly mood that " if he was not
to be allowed to open Parliament himself,
as King of Scotland, he would not degrade
himself by accepting a subordinate position." With his boon companions he rode
off to amuse himself at Leith, taking the
most effective means of giving publicity
to the breach between the Queen and himself.

On the 10th, Mary was at supper with
her half-sister, the Duchess of Argyll, her
Maries, the secretary, and other guests.
Suddenly the curtain covering the en-
trance to a private staircase was pushed
aside and Darnley entered, staring gloomily at the Queen. It was evident that he
had been drinking, and an uneasy feeling
took possession of the company. He sat
down by Mary and put his arm round her
waist. A moment later appeared the

103

ghastly figure of Ruthven, the wizard, his eyes burning with fever, staggering with weakness, but clad in full armour.

Mary, terrified, asked if he had come to kill her.

" No," replied Ruthven, " but we want that rascal David."

Mary had risen to her feet, and the secretary, seeing that some harm was intended him, retreated behind her chair. George Douglas, half-uncle of Darnley, next appeared, followed, to the dismay of the guests, by armed men trooping up the staircase.

Turning to her husband, Mary inquired the meaning of this. Darnley, hesitating, said he knew nothing of it, and Mary ordered the conspirators from her presence. Ruthven entered upon a confused accusation of the secretary, who was clinging to his mistress's gown.

The Douglas war-cry was followed by a rush of men up the staircase. Snatching a dagger, George Douglas stabbed Riccio

QUEEN MARY AT HOLYROOD
By Robert Hope, R.S.A.

THE STORM BURSTS

over the Queen's shoulder ; several men hurled themselves upon him ; the table was upset. The Duchess of Argyll snatched a candle, or the room would have been in darkness. Darnley held Mary while the unfortunate man was dragged from the room. Riccio cried to her for help, and she begged for his life. Kerr of Fawdonside held a loaded pistol to her breast, which was thrust aside by Darnley, and Anthony Standen snatched the dagger of another conspirator which was pointed at the Queen.

The cries of the unfortunate secretary were agonising, and Mary did not cease to beg his life with prayers and tears while he was dragged from the room and dispatched in an adjoining apartment with fifty-six blows of dirks and whingers.

David's cries died into stillness, and the struggles and trampling of feet were succeeded by an ominous hush. A lady of the palace came in and said that the deed had been done by the King's authority.

" Traitor, and son of a traitor," said the Queen, turning to her husband, " is this your gratitude ? " Overcome by her feelings, she fainted away, and on regaining consciousness the first thing that met her eyes was the form of the hated Ruthven, who staggered into the room, excusing himself to the Queen as he sat down in her presence and called for a cup of wine.

Bothwell, Huntly, and Atholl had heard the tumult in another part of the palace, and with the officers of the household were endeavouring to come to the Queen's assistance. A fight took place in the courtyard, and Mary's friends, being overpowered, were fain to make their escape. Twenty-four arquebusiers were posted at the doors of the royal apartments, and the Queen and Darnley found themselves prisoners within their own palace. A report of the tumult having reached Edinburgh, the tocsin was sounded, and the Provost appeared at the gates of Holyrood with a band of armed men demand-

ing to see the Queen. Mary was forbidden with threats to approach the windows, and the conspirators forced Darnley to address the people, assuring them that the Queen was well. The crowd laughed at Mary's unworthy husband, but some of the conspirators assured them that the only trouble had been a quarrel with the French servants of the household, and that the secretary had been put to death because he had been discovered intriguing with the Catholics and with the King of Spain. At this the citizens retired, and all hope of rescue was cut off for the meanwhile.

The night was spent by Mary in pain, and on the following day the Earl of Moray, one of the foremost of the conspirators, entered Holyrood in the guise of a deliverer. Mary, not suspecting the depth of his deception, threw herself into his arms. " If you had been here," she cried, " you would never have allowed me to be treated so cruelly."

107

The tears started from Moray's eyes, but he could not so soon dissociate himself from his late companions, and Mary soon saw that the prospect of a speedy escape depended upon herself. Darnley was now thoroughly alarmed, and it was not hard to convince him of the dangerous position in which his folly had placed both himself and his consort. He persuaded the conspirators to relax their precautions, and communicated with a few faithful followers.

At two in the morning, accompanied only by Margaret Carwood, a waiting-woman of the Queen, Mary and Darnley stole down a secret staircase and through a cellar communicating with the vaults in Holyrood Chapel. A small gate had been left open, and here they found horses in attendance, under the guard of Arthur Erskine, Captain of the Queen's Guard; Stewart, Master of Traquair; and Anthony Standen, Darnley's English equerry. Riding all night, they reached Dunbar by day-

break, and behind the massive walls of the castle were safe from all pursuit.

In spite of fatigue and the dangers which had threatened her, Mary appeared none the worse of her flight. After the astonished warders had lighted a fire, she asked for some eggs, which she cooked herself ; then messengers were sent in all directions to the friends Mary felt she could trust, her letter to the Cardinal of Lorraine being signed "from your niece Marie, a Queen without a Kingdom."

CHAPTER THE TENTH: AN HEIR TO THREE KINGDOMS

KIRKCALDY OF GRANGE

MARY WAS LESS DESTITUTE THAN she supposed. Intelligence of her midnight ride having been received, Bothwell and Huntly came to Dunbar with sixteen hundred armed men, and Atholl, Caithness, the Archbishop of St. Andrews, Lords Hume and Yester were not slow in following their example. Eight thousand men were soon collected, and Mary was able to march to Edinburgh at the head of an army. Moray was pardoned, and those who had taken open part in the late conspiracy fled from the country.

The Queen re-entered Edinburgh in triumph, accompanied by her husband, her faithful lords, and a following of armed men. Avoiding Holyrood, a place of terrible association since the murder, she took up her quarters in the High Street, in a house guarded by cannon. Two of the creatures of Lord Ruthven suffered death for the murder, and the property of the other conspirators was confiscated. Peace having been restored, Mary was inclined to pardon some

II

of the rebels; but Darnley, terrified at the thought of what might be revealed, opposed himself to all clemency. His sole desire now was to escape from the consequences of his folly, and he had the effrontery to appear before the Privy Council and declare that " upon his honour, his loyalty, and his word as a prince, he had never known, advised, ordered, forwarded, or approved of the conspiracy and the violence offered to her Majesty ; he had only consented to the recall of the rebels without knowledge of the Queen, in which he acknowledged that he had done wrong."

A public proclamation to the same effect at the Mercat Cross of Edinburgh aroused the fury of the exiles, who found a means of sending to Mary the " bonds " in which Darnley had undertaken to support them in the plot.

The unfortunate Queen's suspicions were changed into certainty ; she knew now that his public denial had been false, and not only had her husband taken a leading part in the

plot against Riccio, but he had sold her to traitors for the price of power.

The effect was to render her almost broken-hearted. In a letter written to her aunt, the Duchess of Guise, about this time, she says : " I will tell you how much I have changed in a little while ; from being one of the most contented in myself and happy of people, I have now become oppressed with continual trouble and care."

The situation of Darnley was now wretched in the extreme. He must have known that the associates whom he had betrayed were ready for some terrible revenge, and the partisans of Mary showed their contempt and dislike in a manner not to be mistaken. Attended only by a few servants and men-at-arms, he wandered around the capital. An attempt which he made to attach himself to Moray and Argyll was repulsed, and he fell ill from anger and wounded pride.

Weary and harassed, Mary thought seriously of retiring to France, but all other considerations had to be laid aside as the time

of her confinement approached. For the safety of the child who would be heir to the crowns of England and Scotland she endeavoured to make peace among the lords. Bothwell and Huntly had long-standing feuds against Moray, and Atholl and Argyll were at enmity with each other : the Queen induced them to become reconciled and take a solemn engagement to protect the child should she herself not survive his birth. As the hour approached, her angry feelings against her husband became calmer; a reconciliation took place, and she left him a number of legacies in her will, including the ring with which he had married her. Edinburgh Castle was chosen as the place of greatest safety, and Darnley, with the Earls of Moray and Argyll, accompanied the Queen when she retired thither to await her confinement.

In the fortress a son was born on 29th June 1566. Cannons were fired; bonfires on every peak announced the good news throughout the length and breadth of the land;

and James Melville, waiting booted and spurred in the courtyard, rode off with the tidings to Elizabeth.

The entire nation rejoiced at the birth of an heir ; and England, France, and Spain sent congratulations to the Scottish Court. Elizabeth promised to be godmother, and a return of affection was aroused in Catherine de Medici at the news of the birth of a son to the Queen of Scots.

" I was as glad as though she were my own daughter," she wrote to the Duchess of Guise ; " feeling sure that it would be the cause of helping her to arrange her affairs, which the messenger told me were in good order, and that all her subjects were pleased that she had borne a son to her husband. When I asked the messenger for news of the King, he replied that he had not seen him when he left, but the King was very glad. He is so bad that I do not know if he feels as he ought," she wrote, showing insight into Darnley's character ; for the sobering influence of fatherhood proved transient in

117

the case of the hot-tempered and arrogant young man. A few weeks after the birth of her son Mary was obliged to interfere between him and Moray, whom he threatened to kill. The pardon accorded to certain of the conspirators alarmed and irritated him, and in autumn he was forming wild plans for going abroad. The Queen, the Council, and the French Ambassador endeavoured to reason with him, but Darnley remained obdurate, and refusing to give any reason for his conduct, took leave of Mary with vague threats of a final separation.

In October, still at variance with her husband, Mary went to Jedburgh to hold an assize. The Borders were always a seat of disturbance, and the Queen learned that Bothwell, pursuing a noted outlaw named Jock Eliot, had been severely wounded and lay ill in his castle of Hermitage. A week later, the assize being over, Mary, with her brother and all her train, rode from Jedburgh to Hermitage, a distance of eighteen miles, returning on the same day. This long

ride, which her enemies did not fail afterwards to turn to her disadvantage, nearly cost Mary her life ; a fever set in on the following day, and for a week her life was despaired of.

The Bishop of Ross prayed by the Queen's bedside, and calling the Earl of Moray and her lords around her, Mary confided her son to their protection, and entreated them to live at peace with one another during the child's minority. She declared that she died in the Catholic faith, in which she had been brought up, and begged that her brother "would not be over-extreme to such as were of her religion." Her attendants were moved to tears, and the French Ambassador, du Croc, whom she charged with messages for her kinsfolk in France, was indignant at the indifference shown by her husband.

" The King," he wrote, " is at Glasgow, and has not come to this place, although he has received notice, and has had ample time to come had he been willing. His conduct can admit of no excuse."

A contrast to Darnley's conduct was the behaviour of Bothwell, who, as soon as his wound allowed him to travel, had himself transported to Jedburgh in a litter carried by two horses to inquire for his royal mistress. Darnley came at last, but the crisis was over, and after spending one day at Jedburgh he left once more to join his father, the ambitious, shifty Earl of Lennox, the only friend and adviser left to him.

" I could wish to be dead," said the Queen as she returned from the Borders and took up her residence in Craigmillar Castle, near Edinburgh. Darnley had rejoined her for a few days, and had left after further offending the nobility and scandalising the French Ambassador, du Croc, with his insolence and arrogance.

" It is not meet that such a young fool and proud tyrant should reign over us," said her friends, " yet how to be rid of him she sees na outgait."

DAWN AFTER LANGSIDE
By John Lavery, R.S.A.

CHAPTER THE ELEVENTH
A TARDY REPENTANCE

CHAPTER THE ELEVENTH
A TARDY REPENTANCE

ALL PARTIES WERE NOW UNITED against the headstrong youth whose conduct held the country in a state of unrest. Darnley's departure was followed by the "Craigmillar Conference." Maitland of Lethington and Moray, staying in the castle, agreed that it was desirable to recall the Earl of Morton and other lords still banished for the murder of Riccio. Mary's reluctance was well known, and Maitland suggested that the first step would be to obtain a divorce between herself and her husband, who opposed every plan for restoring his late fellow-conspirators.

Early in the morning, the pair sought out the Earl of Argyll and communicated the plan to him. Huntly was then admitted to the council, and finally the confidence of the plotters was extended to Bothwell, the most faithful adherent of the Queen.

All five then sought an audience of Mary, and the subject was broached to her. Maitland alluded to Darnley's folly and perver-

sity, and suggested that the nobles should unite in obtaining a divorce if the Queen would consent to pardon the conspirators in the late plot, a step now rendered necessary by the state of politics.

Maitland was strongly supported by his companions, and Mary was at first inclined to consent, provided the divorce might be obtained without prejudice to her son: "otherwise," she added, "I would rather undergo any torments and run all possible risks." Upon further reflection, she suggested that she herself might retire to France for a time, in the hope that her husband might return to a better frame of mind.

All expressed disapproval, and Lethington said that means would be found for the divorce without affecting the rights of the infant prince, "and albeit my lord of Moray here present be little less scrupulous for a Protestant than your Grace is for a Papist, be assured that he will look through his fingers and behold our doings, saying nothing to the same."

To this ambiguous speech Mary replied :
" I will that ye do nothing through which
any spot may be laid on my honour or conscience ; and therefore, I pray you, rather
let the matter lie in the state that it is, abid-
ing till God of His goodness put remedy
thereto."

Eventually, reflecting that as a Catholic
no lawful divorce could be obtained save on
the ground of consanguinity, which would
render her son illegitimate, Mary refused to
entertain the idea.

To restore peace and safety to the com-
munity, according to Maitland and his associates, it was necessary that the banished
lords should be brought back from England.
To this Darnley remained prime obstacle ;
his influence must therefore be removed
from the Queen, who refused to consent to
a divorce. There still remained a way of
taking away the young man of which few,
in these days, would have been too scrupulous to avail themselves. A bond was drawn
up secretly in which Maitland, Argyll, Hun-

tly, and Bothwell undertook to remove the King by one expedient or another, each engaging to stand by his fellow at the utmost risk of his life and fortune. Moray afterwards swore that he had not subscribed the deed, but he justified Maitland's prediction that he would " look through his fingers " when overtures were sent to the lords, once Darnley's associates, and now his most dangerous enemies.

The splendid preparations for her son's christening were spoiled for Mary by the sullen humour of her husband. Her subjects' consent had been gained for the baptism of the child by the Catholic rite ; the principal nobles were in attendance, and ambassadors came from France, Spain, and England to attend the ceremony, which took place in Stirling Castle on the 17th of December. Elizabeth's emissary was the Earl of Bedford, who brought a gold font for her godson and conciliatory messages for her sister of Scotland.

Darnley came to Stirling, but refused to

be present either at the ceremony or at the magnificent fêtes which followed. " His deportment is incurable," wrote du Croc, " nor can there be ever any good expected of him." " The Queen," he said, " behaved admirably during the baptism, and showed so much earnestness to entertain all the goodly company in the best manner, that this made her forget in a good measure her former ailments. But a few days later she sent for him, and he found her lying on her bed and "weeping sore," complaining of a "grievous pain in her side." " I am much grieved," he added, "for her many troubles and vexations."

At the end of the month the English emissaries returned to their own country, loaded with presents and carrying with them something more important still—the pardon of the Earl of Morton and his associates. This had at last been obtained from Mary through the combined intercessions of Moray, Maitland, Bothwell, and the Earl of Bedford, who added strong representations

from his mistress to the entreaties of her Scottish advisers.

Darnley, to whom the return of the lords had been a veritable sword of Damocles, left Stirling on the same day, without taking leave of the Queen. Among the crazy schemes with regard to which he had let fall hints were one for kidnapping his son and another for becoming a pirate, with the Scilly Isles for his headquarters. The return of his quondam associates, a contingency to which he had looked forward with terror for months, rendered him well-nigh desperate, and once more he joined his father in Glasgow.

What rash step the feather-headed youth might next have taken can only remain a matter of conjecture, but in January he was laid helpless with smallpox. Mary was at Holyrood with her child, and as soon as she received tidings of her husband's plight she sent her French physician, Nau, to his assistance. A few days later she set out herself to visit him, accompanied as far as Callendar by Huntly and Bothwell. Near Glasgow

128

LORD JAMES STEWART, EARL OF MORAY

she was met by Thomas Crawford, a retainer of the Earl of Lennox, bearing his master's excuses for not coming in person to meet her, as he dared not enter her presence because of the "sharp words" she had spoken of him in Stirling.

Contemptuously replying that there was no medicine against fear, Mary dismissed the messenger and proceeded on her way. At the first meeting with her husband she was cold, but Darnley, reduced by sickness and suffering, had entirely changed. He acknowledged his folly and begged for his wife's forgiveness. "I am young," he said, "and you say you have forgiven me divers times. May not a man of my age for lack of counsel, of which I am very destitute, fail twice or thrice, and yet repent and be chastened by experience ?—I crave your pardon and protest that I shall never fail again. I desire no other thing but that we may be together as husband and wife, and if ye will not consent thereto, I desire never to rise from off this bed."

129   I

Mary was "verye pensiffe" for a time, but after some further conversation she gave Darnley her hand and promised that she would love him once more and use him as her husband.

A litter was ready to convey him to Edinburgh, whither the royal pair proceeded by easy stages, to all appearance completely reconciled.

But Darnley's repentance had come too late. Already the meeting had taken place at Whittinghame, where Bothwell and Lethington acquainted the newly-arrived Earl of Morton with the plot against the Queen's husband. Mary, they said, desired him to join with the other conspirators in taking Darnley's life because her husband had been more to blame than they in the murder of Riccio.

Morton, rendered prudent by experience, demanded the Queen's handwriting as a guarantee, but no warrant of Mary's forthcoming, he declined, if his own statement be worthy of credit, to take any active part

in the murder. His approval and indirect assistance were not wanting, and his kinsman and vassal Archibald Douglas, who took a leading part in the tragedy, enjoyed the confidence of his lord both before and after the deed. One after another the Protestant nobles joined the plot, and the consequences of the young King's arrogance and treachery were about to recoil with terrible force upon his own head.

CHAPTER THE TWELFTH

" VENGEANCE IS MINE "

CHAPTER THE TWELFTH
"VENGEANCE IS MINE"

THE YOUNG PRINCE BEING AT HOlyrood, it was inadvisable to risk infection by bringing Darnley thither. Mary herself had proposed Craigmillar as a place of abode during his convalescence, but her husband apparently feeling some uneasiness at being so far from Edinburgh, it was decided to convey him to a small dwelling on the southern boundary of the town.

This house, called Kirk-o'-Field, formed part of what had once been a group of conventual buildings on the high ground now occupied by the Old University. Being recommended by Moray and Lethington on account of its healthy situation, Mary had it fitted up for the reception of her husband, the room underneath his own being reserved for herself. She tended him assiduously, sometimes spending the night in the house, and the young man's convalescence advanced rapidly. Mary appeared to have bestowed upon him the full forgiveness of her generous nature, and Darnley wrote joyfully

135

to his father that complete confidence was restored between them.

The conspirators discovered that the blow must be struck promptly if at all; intelligence of the plot had leaked out, and warnings from France and Spain were on their way to the Queen.

On the 9th of February the Earl of Moray left Edinburgh for St. Andrews despite the entreaties of Mary, who implored him not to leave her. His alleged reason was the illness of his wife, but it was his method always to be absent when any plot was about to be carried out. On the same day Kerr of Fawdonside set out for Edinburgh— the man who had pointed the pistol at the Queen and still remained unpardoned; nothing less than being present at his revenge would satisfy him. The other conspirators were already in their places, Bothwell, Argyll and Huntly spending part of the evening in the young King's room, where he and Mary were discussing plans for the future. During this time it is supposed that Both-

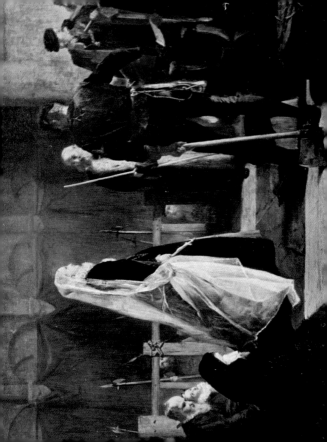

THE EXECUTION OF MARY QUEEN OF SCOTS
By Robert Herdman, R.S.A.

well's servants were carrying the barrels of gunpowder into the cellar underneath the house.

At eleven o'clock, remembering that she had promised to be present at a ball given at Holyrood in honour of the wedding of two of her servants, Mary took leave. Darnley pleaded with her not to leave him, and she promised to return on the following day and spend the night in the house. After some further entreaty Darnley allowed her to go, leaving with him a ring in pledge of her word.

With attendants bearing lighted torches before and behind, Mary set out for Holyrood. Bothwell followed her; but in about an hour's time he left the ball, changed his rich clothes for a plainer suit and then set out once more for Kirk-o'-Field. "The Black Laird" of Ormiston and some of his servants were with him, and a slipper found afterwards proved that Archibald Douglas had been in the house. Other conspirators were there, but their number and identity can only be surmised.

Bothwell entered the house with two men, and remained long enough to light a slow match. Then all three came out quickly, and nineteen or twenty men were seen running rapidly away in the darkness. A poor woman from a cottage hard by caught one of them by the sleeve, but he escaped.

A few minutes later a frightful explosion rent the air, and the house of Kirk-o'-Field was blown from its foundations.

The crime had been carried out in a terrible fashion. When news of the disaster was brought to Bothwell he was in bed, feigning to be asleep. He was unaware that Darnley's body had been found in an orchard some distance from Kirk-o'-Field lying beside that of his valet, neither bearing any traces of the explosion, but with marks of strangulation. Someone had given the alarm, and the two young men had endeavoured to escape, only to be seized by a second body of conspirators, who had surrounded the house unknown to the first, and strangled the King and his servant with the sleeves of their

own shirts. Darnley had been heard crying
for mercy, but the hatred he had inspired
was too great and deep ; there was not the
slightest hope that the murderers would fore-
go their long-wished-for vengeance.

It fell to Bothwell to inform the Queen of
the death of her husband. When the corpse
was brought to Holyrood, Mary looked at
it long and earnestly, but without shedding
a tear, then, taking refuge in Edinburgh
Castle, she gave herself up to the most pro-
found melancholy.

Warnings came, too late, of a plot direct-
ed against herself and her husband. It was
not the intention of the lords to allow suspicion of the murder to fall upon themselves. That Bothwell had been concerned
was evident ; the rash Earl had no gift for
concealment. Having used him as a tool to
strike with, they now proceeded to sacrifice
him ; and the opportunity had come to discredit and remove the Queen.

The terrible event had thrown the people
into a state of nervous terror. The unfor-

tunate victim, lately an object of contempt and dislike, now figured as a martyr, and the question which agitated the minds of all was : Who was the doer of the awful deed ?

Voices were heard at midnight in the streets of Edinburgh denouncing the " shedders of innocent blood," and anonymous placards denounced the Earl of Bothwell as the assassin, the Queen being his accomplice " through the witchcraft of the Lady of Buccleugh."

Mary was warned that her conduct would be liable to the most unfavourable interpretation were prompt measures not taken to discover the murderers. Her chief ministers and the most powerful of the nobility having been concerned in the plot, it is not hard to understand that justice was paralysed. Moray, the foremost man in the Kingdom, remained quietly in Fife after the murder, coming to Edinburgh a month later to dine with Argyll, Lethington, Huntly, and Bothwell himself, who was accused both publicly and privately of being the assassin.

" VENGEANCE IS MINE "

Lennox, the father of the murdered man, was calling loudly for Bothwell's trial. The Borderer collected all his retainers, and never stirred without a numerous following. A few days before the date fixed for the trial, Moray announced his intention of making a long stay in France, whither he went, despite Mary's entreaties. The Earl of Lennox came as far as Stirling with a band of armed men, but at the last moment he declined to proceed, making no further effort to avenge his son.

The trial which now took place was the most amazing farce that ever took place in a court of justice. The Earl of Argyll, one of the conspirators, presided over the court, and the jury was packed with relatives and friends of the accused. Maitland, the Secretary of State, another accomplice, rode beside Bothwell when the Earl mounted his horse, and with about four thousand guards and followers, rode to the Tolbooth to answer to the charge of having murdered the consort of the Queen.

141

But the Earl of Bothwell's audacity failed, the only time we read of such an occurrence. Confronted with his lying accomplices, he looked so downcast and sullen that Ormiston, the " Black Laird," plucked him by the sleeve, urging him in a whisper to hold up his head and look more cheerful.

" I would not yet it were to do," replied Bothwell, brooding upon the murder.

Yet when the inevitable acquittal came, no witnesses having appeared against him, he was able to issue a notice challenging to single combat any one who would accuse him of the murder of the King. Tullibardine, once Bothwell's comrade, his denouncer since the murder, accepted the challenge, but the Earl found some pretext to ignore him.

Two days later Parliament met and, in acknowledgment of Bothwell's " great services," confirmed him in the guardianship of the castle of Dunbar and in his office of Lord High Admiral of Scotland.

The last act of the comedy followed. At

"VENGEANCE IS MINE"

Ainslie's tavern in Edinburgh, on the day Parliament rose, Bothwell gave a supper to the principal nobles of the realm, accomplices and honest men. After the feast, many healths having been drunk and heads being fairly heated, the Earl laid before his guests a bond which he required them to sign.

The contents might well have made the revellers pause, but they discovered that the house was surrounded by armed men. Among the Queen's friends, only one, the Earl of Eglintoun, was sober enough to slip quietly from the table and make his way unperceived through the guards. The lords Herries and Seton remained, hitherto Mary's most faithful supporters.

In the document the signatories were made to declare that Bothwell having been acquitted of the charges brought against him, they bound themselves to defend him " with bodies, heritages, and goods against his privy and public calumniators bypast and to come."

Further, they declared that the widow-

hood of the Queen being a serious danger to the country, they, considering the great merit and the eminent qualities of the Earl of Bothwell, engaged themselves upon their honour and fidelity to further his marriage with their sovereign lady and to risk their lives and goods against any who should oppose it.

Having persuaded or coerced his guests into signing this document, Bothwell, the husband of Lady Jean Gordon, swore that he would marry the Queen, " who wald or who wald not, yea, whether she wald herself or not."

DEATH OF THE REGENT MORAY

CHAPTER THIRTEENTH
"BY FRIENDS DECEIVED, BY FOES BETRAYED"

K

CHAPTER THIRTEENTH
"BY FRIENDS DECEIVED"

THE AIR WAS FULL OF RUMOUR AND unrest when Mary set out to visit her son in Stirling Castle a few weeks after the signing of the bond. On her return, as her little train was approaching Edinburgh, the handful of people was met and surrounded by an armed force of eight hundred men led by the Earl of Bothwell. Riding up to the Queen, Bothwell informed her that she was in the greatest possible danger, and must come with him; then, seizing her bridle-rein, he led her away. Three of her followers— Huntly, Lethington, and Sir James Melville —were allowed to accompany her, and the others were dismissed. Among them was the laird of Borthwick, who, having little confidence in Bothwell's good intentions, put spurs to his horse, and, galloping to Edinburgh, called the citizens to arms.

But eight hundred men were readily able to make their way through hastily aroused and unprepared burghers. Bothwell's followers spurred their horses and outdistan-

147

ced their pursuers. That evening Mary was in the castle of Dunbar, the strongest fortress in Scotland.

On the following day Melville was sent away, having heard Bothwell boast that he had the Queen in his power. Huntly was a weathercock; throughout his career he was to be found now on the Queen's side and now conspiring with her enemies, and he was ready to sacrifice his sister, the Lady Jean Gordon, to his new friendship with Bothwell. Lethington's personal regard for the Queen never weighed for a moment against any political schemes he might have in view. No woman was allowed access to Mary save Lady Coldingham, the sister of Bothwell.

The Queen's own story is the only existing account of what took place within the castle walls. Finding herself a prisoner, she vehemently reproached the Earl for his audacity and ingratitude, using every argument which might induce him to set her free. His demand that she should become

148

his wife she rejected with disdain, when, to her horror and amazement, her captor produced the bond in which the entire nobility of her kingdom, with hardly an exception, friend or foe, pledged their word to use every means in their power to promote the marriage.

The days went past, Bothwell using persuasion and threats, and "never man in Scotland once making a mind to procure our deliverance," Mary became convinced that she was deserted. Force was added to importunities, and when the Queen left Dunbar, a miserable woman, she was accompanied by the Earl of Bothwell and had consented to marry him.

The Lady Jean made no difficulty about the divorce from her hot-tempered husband. The marriage being declared null on the ground of consanguinity, she said nothing of the dispensation which she as a Catholic had obtained from the Pope, but carried the document away with her, some strange scruple preventing her from destroying it

149

even when she became the wife of the Earl of Sutherland, and, on his death, of Ogilvie of Aboyne, the widower of Mary Beaton.

Mary, " the most changed woman of face that ever without extremity of violent sickness we have seen," never stirred without Bothwell, and was always surrounded by a guard, who allowed no one to approach her. The divorce was followed by her marriage in Holyrood at four o'clock in the morning. Bothwell's boon companion, the reprobate Bishop of Orkney, performed the Protestant ceremony, which took place in the council hall and not in the chapel. Mary was in deep mourning, and " there was neither plesur nor pastime usit, as wes wont to be usit quhen princes wes marrit."

On the same day du Croc saw her, and she told him that " she could not rejoice, nor ever would again. All she wished for was death." " Unless God aided," her attendants said, "it was feared that she would become desperate," and she was heard to say that she would stab or drown herself.

150

"BY FRIENDS DECEIVED"

For three weeks she remained in Holyrood, tormented by the jealousy and suspicion of Bothwell, who " made her cause
to shed abundance of salt tears." According
to Melville, many even of Bothwell's supporters believed " that her Majesty would
fain have been quit of him."

The common people were paralysed by
the extraordinary course of events. The
general impression was that Bothwell had
obtained possession of the Queen's person
by violence, and had used force to compel
the marriage. On the other hand, assurances
were published that Mary had forgiven the
Earl and was now acting of her own free
will. Minds were still agitated after the murder, and there was a party who were interes-
ted in fostering the suspicion that Mary had
been concerned in the plot.

Religious and superstitious motives increased the confusion ; the more rigid Cal-
vinists being ready to believe the worst of
an "idolatress," while some found in witchcraft the key to the mystery. It is curious

151

to find how widespread was the belief that the Earl of Bothwell, the student in his Border fortress of the Black Art, had bewitched the Queen with evil spells, and was causing her to work his will.

Meanwhile Lethington, the chameleon, after plotting with Bothwell, had become his open foe, and flying to the Earl of Atholl, roused the clan to the Queen's rescue. The Earl of Morton and Lord Hume raised a body of men under the same pretext, and were joined by the Earl of Mar and Lords Lindsay and Tullibardine, the strangely assorted force being inspired by the most conflicting sentiments regarding their sovereign, but all united in hatred of Bothwell, whose relations with some had been alternately that of the dupe and the bully.

The Earl took refuge with Mary in Borthwick Castle, a fortress of great strength. A hostile army soon surrounded the castle, but, taking advantage of the indecision of the leaders, Bothwell retreated with Mary to Dunbar. In this stronghold he might have

JAMES DOUGLAS, EARL OF MORTON

been secure, but his restless spirit drove him
to action, and in a few days he was with the
Queen at Carberry Hill, near Musselburgh,
the opposing army being encamped on the
other side of a stream.

The insurgents had proclaimed themselves
friendly to the Queen, yet among them were
her notorious enemies. Among the leaders
were men whose names she had seen on the
"bond" pledging them to support Bothwell
in his scheme of marriage, and who had taken
up arms against him once his purpose was ef-
fected. No wonder if Mary hesitated to leave
even Bothwell to trust herself to a body of
rescuers so constituted.

The two armies being separated only by
a short space, the day passed in indecision,
the Queen watching the proceedings from
the hill with Mary Seton beside her. Messages were sent from one side to the other,
and, in the hope of preventing bloodshed,
the French Ambassador, du Croc, rode out
from Edinburgh in the afternoon. The insurgents declared that they had taken up arms
153

solely to avenge the murder of the King and to deliver the Queen. If she would consent to leave " the wretch who held her captive, they were willing to recognise her as their sovereign and serve her on their bended knees as the humblest of her subjects."

The Ambassador having brought this message to Mary, she replied that it looked ill of the lords to act in contradiction to their own signatures after having married her to Bothwell, whom they first acquitted and were now accusing; but if they would ask her pardon, she would be willing to accord it. Bothwell proposed to decide the day by a single combat between himself and any of the rebel leaders, provided the champion were of sufficient rank to meet hand to hand the consort of the Queen. More than one answer came to the challenge, but Bothwell boasted and vapoured, rejecting one after the other.

The Borderer's position was a difficult one. His men were deserting, and the expected reinforcements did not arrive. Still

he showed no sign of fear, and du Croc, hating Bothwell, whom he refused to recognise as the husband of the Queen, was forced to admire his courage, and own that he was a gallant and capable leader.

Finally, after repeated assurances of her safety, Mary surrendered upon condition that all her followers should be allowed to leave the field unharmed. After embracing the Queen, Bothwell galloped off towards Dunbar, and Mary allowed Kirkcaldy of Grange to lead her into the insurgents' camp. She was repeating to the lords the terms upon which she had surrendered when shouts arose of " Burn her! Burn the murderess!"

Seeing the insurgents' banner with a device of Darnley lying dead and her son praying for vengeance, Mary understood that she was accused of husband-murder. Women in those days were burned alive for this crime, and the Queen swooned at the sight, nearly falling from her horse to the ground.

When she came to herself she was conveyed to Edinburgh, led through the streets

155

with the banner borne in front of her, and confined during the night in the house of the Lord Provost. In the morning she called for rescue to the crowd who had assembled beneath her window, and the populace, who had been thrown from one extreme of feeling to the other, began to turn in her favour.

Her captors lodged the Queen in Holyrood that night, and at daybreak she was conveyed secretly from the city and across the river. Her destination was the island fortress of Lochleven, then in the hands of Sir William Douglas, Moray's half-brother, and his mother, Margaret Erskine, once the mistress of James v.

CHAPTER FOURTEENTH: A QUEEN WITHOUT A CROWN

CHAPTER FOURTEENTH
QUEEN WITHOUT A CROWN

HAVING GAINED POSSESSION OF the Queen, the lords were in no hurry to burden themselves with so embarrassing a captive as the Earl of Bothwell. For nearly a fortnight he remained unmolested, then in the name of their sovereign the confederates demanded the surrender of the castle of Dunbar, where he had established his stronghold.

Quitting Dunbar, Bothwell betook himself to the north and found a refuge with his great-uncle, the Bishop of Moray, in Spynie Castle, where, with the Bishop's three wild sons, his proceedings were the reverse of edifying. Eventually, having quarrelled with the young men, the Borderer turned all his kinsmen out of the house, which he manned with his own followers, making himself a terror to the countryside.

The scandal became so great that some steps had to be taken. In August—the encounter at Carberry Hill having taken place in June—the lords sent Tullibardine, now

Bothwell's mortal enemy, and Kirkcaldy of Grange, with orders to pursue the Earl " by sea or land, with fire, sword, and all kind of hostility, and to fence and hold courts of justice wheresoever they shall think fit."

By this time Bothwell had become a pirate and had sailed for the Orkney Islands. Grange and Tullibardine took ship and followed, joined by Bothwell's late friend, the Bishop of Orkney, hot in the chase of his ancient comrade.

In Kirkwall the pursuers found that their prey had fled to Shetland. Sailing north, Bothwell's vessels were sighted, and an exciting chase began among the straits and channels of the archipelago. Grange's vessel was wrecked, but Tullibardine held on in pursuit. Bothwell's ships were overtaken in the open sea, and after three hours of fighting a storm arose, separating the foes and driving the pirate vessels on to the coast of Norway.

Suspicion being aroused in the port whither the ships put in for repair, Bothwell at-

JAMES VI. AS A BOY.

tempted to carry matters off with a high hand, but his battered and threadbare appearance accorded ill with his assertion that he was the husband of the Queen of Scotland and supreme governor of that country. Inquiries were set on foot, and the Earl was conveyed to Denmark, where he was thrown into prison. Here he remained while the rulers of the two countries conferred with one another, and his old associates showed no great anxiety to bring so dangerous a prisoner back to his native land.

Years went by, and the fiery Borderer was still importuning the King of Denmark and writing the boastful *Mémoire* intended to influence that monarch in his favour. For such a nature no punishment could have been devised greater than to let him fret out the rest of his days in captivity, for the Earl was never to escape from the trap into which he had fallen through his rash confidence in those more apt than himself in the art of deception. After ten years of captivity he died in the Danish fortress of Dragsholm, his

L

mummied corpse, or one answering to his description, being found in a vault under the little church of Faarvejle, the broad skull and hawk-like features undergoing the indignity of photography some twenty years ago.

The Queen having been consigned to a dungeon in the island fortress of Lochleven, the lords had some difficulty in accounting to the European powers for their treatment of her. Elizabeth of England, seriously alarmed by the example to her own subjects, took up the cause of her "sister" with warmth. "Where is my lord of Lethington's natural bond towards her who hath tied him so largely and so bountifully!" she cried. "Fie upon ingratitude!" Throgmorton was sent to Scotland with instructions to use all efforts to obtain Mary's freedom, and the young King of France, Charles IX., who had always loved his sister-in-law, was eager to send an army for her deliverance.

For a time the lords tried to represent themselves as having acted entirely in Mary's interests. "Do you not see that it does not

lie within my powers to do that which I would fainest do," said Lethington to Throgmorton, " which is to save the Queen, my mistress, in estate, person, and in honour?" He affected to show that it was only in captivity that Mary's life was safe from the people, stirred by the sermons of the preachers to regard their Sovereign as a murderess and idolatress, and from her enemies among the lords.

These excuses failing to convince the Queen's advocates, the confederates were driven to justify themselves upon another plea.

It was then that the much controverted Casket Letters were produced, intercepted, it was said, by the Earl of Morton, who discovered a servant of Bothwell's conveying a silver box belonging to Mary from Edinburgh Castle. The casket, being forced open in the presence of Morton, Lethington, Atholl, and Archibald Douglas, was found, according to them, to contain a series of sonnets written by Mary to Bothwell and

163

breathing the most ardent affection for the Earl. In the casket were also discovered letters written while Mary was in attendance upon the sick Darnley and proving her to be in a league with the murderer, luring her husband to Edinburgh in accordance with a scheme of villainy devised by them both.

Among the many disputed points in the story of the Queen of Scots, none has been more fiercely controverted than the genuineness or the reverse of the Casket Letters. If genuine, Mary's guilt was only paralleled by her folly, and one of the most tender-hearted and generous of women had broken down in character so far as to become cruel and treacherous at a most difficult period of her career—one of the strangest moral tragedies in the world's story.

The whole history, however, of the documents tends to discredit them from the time they first appear in the hands of men driven to find some means of diverting suspicion from themselves. The Queen was never allowed to see the writings upon which

her enemies based their charges against her, and she publicly and expressly denied having written "anything concerning that matter to any living creature.

" And if any such writings be, they are false and feigned, forged and invented by themselves ; . . . and there are divers in Scotland, both men and women, that can counterfeit my handwriting, and write the like manner of writing which I use as well as myself, and principally such as are in company with themselves." No originals of the incriminating letters, alleged to be in Mary's handwriting and signed by her, were forthcoming; all that was ever produced being copies, unsigned and undated.

If it is true, as they alleged, that the lords came into possession of clear proofs of Mary's complicity on the 20th of June, their conduct immediately afterwards is extraordinary. On the 30th June his late associates issued a summons in her name against the Earl of Bothwell, charging only him with the murder and accusing him of the Queen's

abduction. " He beset her Majesty's way, took and ravished her most noble persoun, and led the same with him to Dunbar Castle, detaining her, and for fear of her life making her promise to marry him." To Elizabeth they declared that Bothwell had compelled Mary to become his wife " by fear, force, and other extraordinary and more unlawful means," yet at this time they were privately circulating reports of the incriminating letters to discredit the Queen with the common people and taking steps to ensure that the rumour should reach France, Spain, and the Papal Court. So far their endeavour had been to throw the sole blame of the murder upon the Queen and Bothwell, and it was only after they had begun to quarrel among themselves and accuse each other of complicity that it came out that hardly a nobleman in the kingdom but had been implicated.

On the 25th of June messengers arrived in Lochleven : the fanatical Lord Lindsay, Ruthven, the son of Darnley's murderer,

and Sir Robert Melville, the brother of James Melville, the Queen's friend. Being shown into Mary's presence, they produced documents in which the Queen was made to abdicate in favour of her son, appointing the Earl of Moray as Regent with a council to carry on the government until he should return from France. Two notaries who accompanied them were authorised to obtain the Queen's signature in due form to the deeds.

Mary refused to sign the papers, but the lords had chosen as their ambassadors two bigots to whom the Catholic Queen was an idolatress without principle or conscience, to be coerced or destroyed if she opposed her will to that of the Chosen. Ruthven and Lindsay commanded and threatened, and Melville, standing by, begged the Queen to yield for the time being.

Lindsay, swearing that the lords would be compelled to cut her throat, forced the pen into Mary's hand and made her sign. The notaries then proceeded to read the

167

documents aloud, requiring the Queen's assent, to which she replied that promises obtained by constraint not being binding she would keep them no longer than during her captivity.

Finally, the Laird of Lochleven being absent and the entire household having shown themselves favourable to Mary, the envoys affected to discover that the captive was not in strict enough confinement. Amid the protests of her guardians she was removed to a dark tower and secured behind an iron gate. Four days later her infant son was crowned in Stirling, and Mary was no longer Queen of Scotland.

CHAPTER THE FIFTEENTH
A QUEEN'S FORLORN HOPE

CHAPTER THE FIFTEENTH
A QUEEN'S FORLORN HOPE

BY THIS TIME MARY HAD BEEN Queen of two countries and twice a widow; her life and person had been the subject of murderous plots, and she now lay in prison, discrowned and in peril of a fiery death, yet she had not reached the age of five-and-twenty. In her hope was hard to extinguish; the Queen of England had sent sympathising messages, and Lethington, rallying once more to her side, found a means of conveying into Mary's hands a small gold representation of the mouse gnawing the lion's bonds, a token that her friends were active on her behalf.

In imprisoning her in Lochleven Castle her foes had reckoned without taking into account the charm of the Queen's personality. Within a few weeks she had won every inmate of the fortress to a more or less enthusiastic regard for her. The rigour of her captivity was modified, and she was allowed the services of Mary Seton and of a waiting-maid named Marie Courcelles. Her gaoler

171

himself took her on hawking and fishing ex-
peditions, and even old Lady Douglas, who
persisted in regarding herself as the lawfully-
married widow of the late King James, and
Mary as an interloper, was beguiled into
tolerance. The laird's young daughter and
niece, who took turns in sleeping with Mary
to prevent an escape during the night, could
only be satisfied with a promise that the
Queen would take them with her should she
ever be set free from captivity.

Of more consequence still was the devotion of Sir William's youngest brother,
George Douglas, a youth of about twenty,
who was banished from the island on suspicion of carrying messages between the
Queen and her supporters. A threat to have
him hanged if ever he should set foot again
in Lochleven lost Moray the allegiance of his
half-brother, who vowed that from thence-
forward he would support the cause of the
royal captive. A foundling lad, Willie, page
to the laird, who had bestowed upon him
the family name of Douglas, becoming

boyishly attached to the Queen, letters were easily conveyed from the island to George, who came and went in secret, and transmitted all messages to the loyal lords.

There was probably little suspicion in the minds of the Regent or Sir William as spring advanced and the Queen's friends were gathering their forces. Whether the spirit of the nation was less gloomy than in later generations or it was the Queen's natural gaiety that infected her companions it is hard to say, but the inmates of the island castle seemed to be bearing their troubles lightly. We read of Mary and her attendants indulging in games of " follow-my-leader" in the garden, leaping walls, and secretly trying whether it would be possible to overcome these obstacles in the hurry and precipitation of a flight. A mock siege of the castle took place, old Lady Douglas unbending so far as to be among the defenders while the attacking party were supposed to be fighting for the deliverance of the Queen from captivity.

173

At last came the day when all had been secretly arranged for Mary's flight. It was the 2nd of May, and a feast was held, Willie Douglas, as Abbot of Unreason, presenting each member of the company with a green branch, and playfully making the Queen promise to follow him for the remainder of the day whithersoever he should lead her. In the afternoon a body of men was seen passing through the hamlet of Kinross, and a pear-shaped pearl being brought to the Queen as a token, she understood that all was ready.

Changing her dress for a red kirtle and a country-woman's mantle and hood, Mary caused Marie Courcelles to do the same, and waited while Willie Douglas stole the keys of the castle. Then, leaving Mary Seton to occupy the attention of her guardians, Mary and her attendant boldly passed through the crowd of retainers in the court-yard and followed Willie through the great gate, which he locked behind them. A boat was in readiness, and they were rowed across

by the faithful Willie, who threw the keys
" to the kelpies' keeping " in the lake.
George Douglas was in the village with
horses, and six or seven miles had been put
between the fugitives and the castle before
the alarm was raised. Pursuit was hopeless, and by midnight Mary was across the
Forth and safe within the walls of West
Niddrie House, the residence of Lord Seton,
sixty miles from Lochleven.

The Queen's first act was to issue a proclamation revoking the promise extorted
from her in captivity. Letters were sent
asking for reinforcements from the King of
France, and a message was dispatched to
Elizabeth with a ring which the English
Queen had sent to her sister of Scotland as
a pledge that she would stand by her in
need. On the following day she mounted
her horse and set out with all her following
for Hamilton, where she was joined by fresh
reinforcements. In a few days six thousand men had joined her standard, all inspired by chivalrous loyalty for the Queen,

175

and led by Argyll, Huntly, Lord Claud Hamilton, the Earls of Eglintoun, Cassilis, Rothes, Sutherland, and Lords Fleming, Livingston, Ogilvie, Herries, Seton, and Maxwell. Nine bishops were under her banner and a large number of gentlemen.

Full of hope, the Queen set out for the west of Scotland, and encountered her brother's forces at Langside, near Glasgow. The Hamiltons, eager for the fight, would not wait for Huntly's reinforcements, but compelled the Earl of Argyll to give instant battle.

The Queen's brother-in-law was a poor leader to oppose to the steady generalship of Moray and Kirkcaldy of Grange. From her position on the slope of a hill above Langside Mary beheld the defeat of her followers, and terror at the prospect of falling into the hands of her enemies took possession of her. Remembering the ignominy of her capture after Carberry Hill, she took horse with her ladies and fled from the field, accompanied by George and Willie Douglas and a few followers. Lord Herries led the

party by unfrequented ways to the Borders, where the principal families were still loyal to the Queen. For three nights, Mary wrote to the Cardinal of Lorraine, she was like the owls, travelling through a country unknown to her, the wild moorlands of Galloway. Their horses having become exhausted, the fugitives left them and pressed forward on foot, sleeping by daytime beneath rocks and overhanging banks. Her first place of refuge was Lord Herries' seat in Dumfriesshire, whence she fled to Dundrennan Abbey. Here a council was held with a few loyal subjects. Lord Herries implored the Queen to fortify herself in some Border keep, and wait for her followers to rally and join with the Maxwells, the Scotts, and the Kerrs, all of whom were devoted to her service.

But Mary had not forgotten the threats of a death at the stake, a prospect which dismayed even her high spirit. Either France or England was open to her as a refuge until her friends had time to rise. France was a long way off, and England lay

only across the Solway. Her sister-queen had sent loving messages to her in captivity, and an envoy had come bringing back the ring which Mary had sent to Elizabeth and a message bidding her take heart and seek a refuge if she wished in England until her own country became more tranquil.

It was in vain that Mary's friends argued and implored ; her impulsive nature asserted itself once more to her undoing.

A rude fishing boat was brought, and in it she embarked, with George and Willie Douglas, her waiting-maid, and Lord Herries, who begged her on his knees to give up the rash scheme.

As the boat left the shore a last appeal was made by the Archbishop of St. Andrews. Plunging waist-deep into the water, he grasped the gunwale and addressed a passionate warning to the Queen, begging her, if she valued her life and liberty, to turn back.

But he might have addressed his warning to the wind and waves. Fatal obsession was urging Mary to her doom.

CHAPTER THE SIXTEENTH
"JE NE SUIS PLUS CE QUE JE FUS"

CHAPTER THE SIXTEENTH
"PLUS CE QUE JE FUS"

EVERY STEP WHICH MARY TOOK upon English ground but served to entangle her further in the toils from which there was no escape. Landing as a private person, her disguise was soon penetrated, and the story of her romantic flight becoming known, both gentry and common people flocked to see the young Queen of Scots. In the absence of Lord Scrope, Warden of the Western Marches, his deputy, Mr. Lowther, came to receive her, and with a number of local gentlemen, accompanied her as far as Carlisle.

From this town Mary addressed a grateful letter to Elizabeth, unaware that her charm was doing its worst for herself and for hundreds among those who thronged to welcome her. The north of England being still to a large extent Catholic, the Queen of Scots was regarded by many of the people as their rightful sovereign, and the enthusiasm aroused by her personality became alarming to the ministers of Elizabeth. "Surely she is a rare woman," wrote Sir Francis Knollys

after visiting her in Carlisle, "for as no flattery can abuse her, so no plain speech seems to offend her if she thinks the speaker be an honest man." She had thrown herself upon the generosity of Elizabeth, and a memorandum of Lord Burghley's sums up the situation. "She is to be helped, because she came willingly into the realm upon trust of the Queen's majesty. She trusted upon the Queen's majesty's help because she had in her troubles received many messages to that effect. She is not lawfully condemned, because she was first taken by her subjects, by force kept in prison, put in fear of her life, charged with the murder of her husband, and not admitted to answer thereto, neither in her own person nor her advocate, before them which in Parliament did condemn her."

Yet this conviction did not prevent his taking advantage of Mary's rashness. "The surety of the Queen of Scots is first to be considered," he wrote, "that by no practice she should be conveyed out of the realm."

Her ministers soon made Elizabeth repent

of the generous impulse which had prompted her to offer a refuge to the Queen of Scots. Against her better judgment she yielded, an error which cost her nineteen years of anxiety and ended in the crime which has obscured the glory of her reign.

Still regarding her great cousin as a friend, Mary consented to an investigation of the reports concerning herself and that " the men who had deprived her of the crown and of everything else besides, should be made to explain by what authority they had exercised such extraordinary powers." This was followed by her removal from Carlisle to Bolton Castle in Yorkshire—a prisoner. The Conference begun at York was transferred to Westminster. Elizabeth's commissioners were the Duke of Norfolk, the Earl of Sussex, and Sir Ralph Sadleir, who had seen the Scottish Queen in her cradle at Stirling. Among those appearing against Mary were her brother the Earl of Moray, Morton, and Adam Bothwell, the notorious Bishop of Orkney. Regarding her adversaries Sussex wrote dryly that " if

183

they accuse her of the murder by producing of her letters, she will deny them, and accuse the most of them of manifest consent to the murder, hardly to be denied, so as upon the trial on both sides her proofs will judicially fall best out, as it is thought."

Mary's demand for an interview with Elizabeth and to be present at the inquiry was disregarded. The Casket Letters were produced — forged, her defenders maintained, or garbled "in substantious clauses." The Queen was not allowed to see them, and denied their authenticity. Morton swore to the truth of his story of their finding, and Moray laid on the table a book of "Articles containing certain conjectures, presumptions, likelihoods and circumstances" to the discredit of his sister.

The inquiry dragged on its interminable length, "the affirming and denying on both sides," according to the Duke of Norfolk, "surpassing belief." Attempts were made to intimidate Mary into resigning her crown, but she remained steadfast, declaring that

her last words would be those of a Scottish Queen. Finally the inquiry was "huddled up," nothing having been proved or even properly investigated, but everything being done to spread abroad accusations discrediting the Queen in the eyes of the world.

A definite conclusion was avoided. Moray and his allies were informed that "there had been nothing sufficiently produced nor shown by them against the Queen their Sovereign, whereby the Queen of England should conceive or take any evil opinion of the Queen her good sister for anything yet seen." Yet on the other hand Mary's supporters were told that under the painful circumstances of the case Elizabeth was unable to admit the Scottish Queen to her presence—and their mistress was detained in England.

Mary was twenty-five at the time of her flight ; "one long captivity" sums up the story of the rest of her life. For nineteen years she was transferred from prison to prison. Bolton Castle was followed by Tutbury. The northern counties having risen in her favour

185

she was removed to Sheffield, and spent fourteen years under the guardianship of the Earl of Shrewsbury and his termagant wife. Chartley, Tixall, Chatsworth, were all in turn her prisons.

Still she remained the same : ardent, impulsive, hopeful ; full of illusions in spite of repeated disappointment, and confident in the will of her friends to help her. For some years a party held out for her in Scotland, and their reverses were "as grievous as any death could be to her." An added bitterness was the knowledge that her son was in the hands of those who trained him to regard her as an enemy. By what seemed a refinement of malice, his guardians had placed the young James in the charge of Buchanan, her own tutor in happier days, who was now denouncing her in his *Detectio*.

One after another, the Regents of Scotland came to violent ends—Murray falling under the assassin's bullet ; Lennox in civil strife ; Morton on the scaffold. The country was no more peaceful than during her own

troubled reign, yet freedom under any conditions was preferable to captivity. Hope could only cease with her life; she wrote endless appeals to Elizabeth, and letter after letter was sent to her friends and kinsfolk in France and to the King of Spain, who, she was convinced, only awaited their opportunity of interfering on her behalf.

The years rolled on, and only brought increased severity in her confinement. Her health suffered from want of exercise and from the cold and damp of her prisons; she became crippled with rheumatism, and her hair turned prematurely grey.

Many a time did Elizabeth and her ministers repent the blunder which they had made in detaining the Queen of Scots to be a rallying-point for the malcontents of the country, for the Catholics who saw in her their rightful Sovereign, and for all of the race of Don Quixote. Plot succeeded plot for her deliverance, and it was as dangerous to keep her in England as to let her go.

The situation became untenable, "and

a short and sharp cure the only solution."
Once the destruction of the Scottish Queen
was determined upon, it was not difficult to
involve her in a snare. Her gaolers only had
to forward the letters written to her by some
of her would-be rescuers and intercept her
replies.

The Babington conspiracy fell out very
opportunely for the English ministers. A
group of young enthusiasts, mostly Catholics, with one Anthony Babington at their
head, and a fanatic named Ballard as their
moving spirit, formed themselves into a
brotherhood for the freeing of the Queen of
Scots. Spies were introduced among them.
The proceedings of the band were carefully
watched, while Ballard aroused the young
men to a fervour of devotion, and a spy named Giffard encouraged them to over-confid-
ence. Letters passing between the brotherhood and the royal captive were intercepted
and tampered with by a forger before being
sent to Walsingham.

When the plot had been suffered to con-

tinue for some months, the time came to strike. The unfortunate young men were arrested upon a charge of high treason, tortured, and put to death.

To her amazement, Mary was arrested and charged with having conspired against the life of the Queen of England. Her servants were sent away, while her coffers were ransacked for incriminating papers and her money and jewels taken from her. A few days later she was conveyed to Fotheringay, a fortress which was afterwards razed to the ground in the vain hope of effacing the memory of what took place within its walls.

CHAPTER SEVENTEENTH
"THE VASTY HALLS OF DEATH"

CHAPTER SEVENTEENTH
"VASTY HALLS OF DEATH"

SOME WEEKS AFTER HER ARREST the Commissioners came to Fotheringay to try the Queen of Scots. Among them were the Archbishop of Canterbury, the Lord Chancellor, Burghley, Walsingham, Leicester, who had been a suitor for her hand, Sir Ralph Sadleir, and Sir Christopher Hatton.

On the morning of the 25th of October the Court opened in the great hall of the Castle. Mary entered leaning on the arm of Andrew Melville, her master of the household, and supported by her physician, Bourgoing.

After scanning the array of faces she observed, "So many counsellors, and not one for me."

She had been refused the help of counsel, but was allowed to speak in her own defence. She began by denying that Elizabeth had any jurisdiction over her, the Queen of an independent country, and said that she only consented to appear in order to clear her name from the charge made against her. She denied having entered into any conspir-

193   N

acy against the life of Elizabeth, although she acknowledged having used every means to regain her own liberty, and reminded the Court that she had warned the Queen that she would accept aid to that end from foreign princes. Finally she asked why the witnesses had been put to death without first having been confronted with her.

For two days Mary defended her life and reputation before her thirty-six judges, but the conclusion was a foregone one. It was not justice which her accusers wanted, but the one means of escape from a dilemma. " May God pardon you," said the Queen, in taking leave of the Court after all hope had been extinguished, "and keep me from having to do with you all again."

In November she was told that she must die.

" Madame," she wrote to Elizabeth, " I thank God with all my heart that it pleases Him to put an end, through you, to the weary pilgrimage of my life. I do not ask that it should be prolonged, having had too much

194

experience of its bitterness." She entreated the Queen of England to grant three requests: first, that her servants might be allowed to convey her body to France, to be interred in sacred ground beside that of her " good mother"; secondly, that she might not be put to death in secret; and her third petition was that her faithful dependents might be allowed to depart in safety whither they pleased, and be permitted to retain the small legacies which she was able to leave them.

" I conjure you, Madame," ran the letter, " by the blood of Jesus Christ, by our relationship, by the memory of Henry VII., our common ancestor, and by the title of Queen, which I bear to my death, not to refuse these reasonable demands and to assure me of this by a word in your hand. Then I shall die as I have lived, your affectionate sister and prisoner, *MARIE, REYNE*."

As time went on and the carrying out of the sentence was delayed, she wrote once more to Elizabeth referring to her dread of being made away with by poison or in secret.

This fear was not without foundation, for an attempt was made to induce Sir Amias Paulet to have her assassinated in prison. To the credit of the stern Puritan be it recorded that Sir Amias rejected the proposal in a letter full of grief and indignation.

More than two months passed in suspense, Elizabeth being unable to make up her mind to face the storm which would be aroused throughout Europe by her daring to bring a fellow-sovereign to the block. In Mary, hope gave way to resignation. Her letters are full of courage, showing constancy and affection towards the friends of her youth and love for her son, which became mingled with bitterness as the conviction dawned upon her that her fate was leaving him indifferent. Again and again there recurs the note of anxiety for the welfare of the little following who had remained faithful to her through all changes of fortune. She commended them to the King of France, and desired that her body might be buried in Rouen beside her mother and her heart laid in the grave of Francis.

" VASTY HALLS OF DEATH "

Elizabeth's ministers were more firm than herself; the representations of the French and Spanish envoys were disregarded, and a haughty reply was sent to the tardy remonstrances of the young King James. The Queen's consent was almost wrung from her, and on 7th February 1587 the Earls of Kent and Shrewsbury appeared at Fotheringay. Together with her two keepers they were shown into the presence of the Queen of Scots, and informed her that she was to prepare for death on the following day. With great calmness, Mary thanked them for the news, and laying her hand on a Testament, swore that she had never taken part in any conspiracy against the life of Elizabeth.

The Earl of Kent, a harsh bigot, discovering that the volume was a "Popish" one, interrupted her to declare that "an oath taken upon that Testament was as valueless as the book itself."

"According to my belief," replied the Queen, with dignity, "it is the true Testament. Would you, my lord, give more credit

to my oath if I swore upon your version, in which I do not believe ? "

Once more she begged that she might be allowed the services of a chaplain, and upon Kent's refusal, inquired at what hour the sentence would be carried out.

"At eight o'clock in the morning," replied the Earl of Shrewsbury ; and the Queen's servants with tears and cries implored the envoys that their mistress might be allowed a little longer time.

Shrewsbury had to reply that no delay was possible, and the deputation withdrew, leaving the Queen with her sorrowing attendants.

" My children," said Mary, "this is no time to weep," and she reminded them that there was much to do in the short time which remained.

That night she made her will, dividing what remained of her possessions among her kinsfolk, friends, and servants. She wrote a long letter to the King of France, informing him that she was about to be executed

on the following morning, like a criminal, upon a charge of which she was innocent, and begging him to pray for her soul and take her poor servants under his protection. She bade farewell to her attendants, charging them with her last messages to her son.

It was now two o'clock in the morning, and the Queen lay down and slept while the sound of hammering came from the hall where the scaffold was being erected. At six she rose and called her ladies to dress her " as for a festival," in a black satin bodice and train, a crimson petticoat, and a cap and veil of white—the robes of a Queen-Dowager of France. A message was sent to her chaplain, begging him to pray for her ; and last farewells were taken of all.

It was still early, and the Queen and her ladies sat by a wood fire which was burning in her room, Mary " speaking to her women and consoling them, rather than they her ; telling them that the joys of this world were nothing, as her fate would show to all, from the greatest upon the earth to the least : she,

199

who had been Queen of the kingdoms of France and Scotland, the one through inheritance and the other by fortune, and having triumphed in all honours and greatness, now being delivered into the hands of the executioner, although innocent. The thought of her innocence was her consolation ; she was being made to die for the sake of the good and holy Catholic religion, which she would not abandon with her latest breath, since she had been baptized in it. She desired no other glory after her death than that they (her attendants) should announce her firmness throughout France when they returned to that country, as she hoped they would do; and although she knew that it would cause them much grief of heart to see her upon the scaffold, she desired that they should be witnesses of her death, well knowing that she could have none more faithful to relate what was about to take place."*

She added some last recommendations to her letter to the King of France, then all went

* Brantôme.

into the oratory and remained a long time in prayer.

When the summons came, her servants clustered around her, weeping. Melville, the Queen's faithful steward, brother of Sir James and Sir Robert, who had known her all her life, met her at the door. Flinging himself at her feet, the old man lamented the hard fate which would make him the bearer of the tidings of her death to Scotland.

"Weep not, good Melville," said the Queen; "to-day thou shalt see Mary Stewart delivered from all her cares." With tears she entrusted him with a last message for her son; then saying, "Adieu, good Melville, until we meet in the next world; and pray for me," she passed on her way. Her limbs being crippled with rheumatism, she was unable to walk without assistance. At the door of the hall she begged that her women might be allowed to accompany her, but Kent refused on the ground that they would disturb the company by their cries and lamentations. Mary undertook that they would be silent,

and Shrewsbury intervening on her behalf, she was allowed their services.

About two hundred people were gathered in the hall when the Queen of Scots entered. A flush was on her cheeks; the company were surprised at finding her still so beautiful, and she bore herself with dignity and composure.

" Help me," she said to Melville, when about to mount the scaffold ; " it is the last service I shall receive of you." Then she sat down and listened with perfect composure to the reading of the death-warrant.

The Dean of Peterborough came forward and appealed to her to change her religion at the last moment, and " repent of her former wickedness." Mary repulsed him with gentle firmness, and prayed aloud with her attendants in Latin while the others prayed in English—the religious differences being irreconcilable.

After a last prayer Mary rose and called her women, who broke into tears and lamentations. " Ne criez pas," she said : " j'ai promis pour vous ; " and when they forced

themselves to be silent, she kissed and blessed them, then with their help laid aside her veil and her black gown, making a last signal of farewell to Melville and the others, who groaned and prayed on a front bench.

Her petticoat was red, and under the gown was a crimson bodice. She drew a pair of crimson sleeves over her white arms, and stood in the gloom of the winter morning a brave figure clad all in red.

What strange undercurrent of feeling prompted this attire can be dimly understood. The Queen of Scots faced death with an undaunted spirit, gallant and romantic like the race from which she sprang; protesting against the injustice of her doom and confident in the verdict of those she loved and of posterity.

The spectators were profoundly impressed by her courage ; they broke into tears when she knelt down and groped for the block, saying, "Into Thy hands, O Lord, I commend my spirit." Her head was struck from her shoulders ; the executioner held it up with

the words, "God save the Queen," and the Dean of Peterborough cried, "So perish all the Queen's enemies!"

None save the Earl of Kent replied "A-men." Shrewsbury was shedding tears, and the rest of the spectators were silent.

ROMANTIC LIVES

A series of monographs, handsomely and artistically produced, of the lives of such beautiful and famous women and chivalrous men, whose careers provide to the present-day reader possibly the most fascinating stories in history. Each volume is written by a recognised authority on his subject, and contains illustrations in colour and in imitation photogravure of the best portraits and pictures relating to the period.

With many Illustrations in Colour, in Gravure-tint, and in Collotype. Crown 8vo, buckram, with mounted illustrations, **5s. net** ; bound in velvet Persian and boxed, **7s. 6d. net** ; vellum, **10s. 6d. net.**

NELL GWYN

By CECIL CHESTERTON. With 4 Illustrations in Colour and 16 in Gravure-tint.

The story of Nell Gwyn, who won the heart of King Charles II, is presented in this volume by Mr. Chesterton in a most attractive and readable manner.

LADY HAMILTON

By E. HALLAM MOORHOUSE, Author of " Nelson's Lady Hamilton." With 4 Illustrations in Colour and 19 in Gravure-tint.

Emma Hamilton is one of the most picturesque feminine figures on the stage of history by reason of the great beauty which caused her to play such a conspicuous part in the events of Europe in her day.

MARIE ANTOINETTE

By FRANCIS BICKLEY, Author of "King's Favourites." With 4 Illustrations in Colour and 16 in Gravure-tint.

Marie Antoinette stands out as one of the tragic figures of history. How her brilliant, extravagant court and her light-hearted intrigues culminated in the storm of the French Revolution, and her tragic end on the scaffold, is a most fascinating study.

MARY, QUEEN OF SCOTS

By HILDA T. SKAE, Author of " The Life of Mary, Queen of Scots." With 16 Illustrations in Colour and 8 Portraits in Collotype.

PRINCE CHARLIE

By WILLIAM POWER. With 16 Illustrations in Colour and 8 Portraits in Collotype.

T. N. FOULIS, PUBLISHER, 91 GREAT RUSSELL STREET LONDON, W.C.; 15 FREDERICK STREET, EDINBURGH